CONVENTION
SALES AND SERVICES

CONVENTION
SALES AND SERVICES

By
William Lever

DISCOVERY PUBLISHING HOUSE PVT. LTD.
NEW DELHI-110 002

Published by:
Tilak Wasan
DISCOVERY PUBLISHING HOUSE PVT. LTD.
4831/24, Prahlad Street, Ansari Road
Darya Ganj, New Delhi-110002 (India)
Phone : +91-11-23279245, 43764432
Fax : +91-11-23253475
E-mail : parul.wasan@gmail.com
discoverypublishinghouse@gmail.com
info@discoverypublishinggroup.com
web : www.discoverypublishinggroup.com

First Edition: **2011**
ISBN: 978-81-8356-933-0

Convention: ***Sales and Services***

Printed at:
Mehra Offset Press
Delhi

Preface

A convention, in the sense of a meeting, is a gathering of individuals who meet at an arranged place and time in order to discuss or engage in some common interest. The most common conventions are based upon industry, profession, and fandom. Trade conventions typically focus on a particular industry or industry segment, and feature keynote speakers, vendor displays, and other information and activities of interest to the event organizers and attendees. Professional conventions focus on issues of concern to the profession and advancements in the profession. Such conventions are generally organized by societies dedicated to promotion of the topic of interest.

In the technical sense, a convention is a meeting of delegates or representatives. The 1947 Newfoundland National Convention is a classic example of a state-sponsored political convention. More often, organizations made up of smaller units, chapters, or lodges, such as labor unions, honorary societies, and fraternities and sororities, meet as a whole in convention by sending delegates of the units to deliberate on the organization's common issues. This also applies to a political convention, though in modern times the common issues are limited to selecting a party candidate or party chairman. In this technical sense, a congress, when it consists of representatives, is a convention.

Sales and marketing generates the strategy that underlies sales techniques, business communication, and business developments.[1] It is an integrated process through which companies build strong customer relationships and create value for their customers and for themselves. Marketing is used to identify the customer, to satisfy the customer, and to keep the customer. Some hotels offer meals as part of a room and board arrangement. In the United Kingdom, a hotel is required by law to serve food and drinks to all guests within certain stated hours. In Japan, capsule hotels provide a minimized amount of room space and shared facilities.Hotels are also classified by service type ranging for all-inclusive full-service resorts that cater to vacationers to small limited service hotels that cater to transient business travelers. In this regard, it should be noticed that lower classification or lower star rating does not necessarily mean that the hotel lacks standard.

—Author

Contents

1

An Introduction to Convention Sales and Services

A convention, in the sense of a meeting, is a gathering of individuals who meet at an arranged place and time in order to discuss or engage in some common interest. The most common conventions are based upon industry, profession, and fandom. Trade conventions typically focus on a particular industry or industry segment, and feature keynote speakers, vendor displays, and other information and activities of interest to the event organizers and attendees. Professional conventions focus on issues of concern to the profession and advancements in the profession. Such conventions are generally organized by societies dedicated to promotion of the topic of interest. Fan conventions usually feature displays, shows, and sales based on pop culture and guest celebrities. Science fiction conventions traditionally partake of the nature of both professional conventions and fan conventions, with the balance varying from one to another. Conventions also exist for various hobbies, such as gaming or model railroads.

Conventions are often planned and coordinated, often in exacting detail, by professional meeting and convention planners, either by staff of the convention's hosting company or by outside specialists. Most large cities will have a convention center dedicated to hosting such events. The term MICE - meetings Incentives Conventions and Exhibitions - is widely used in Asia as a description of the industry. The Convention ("C") is one of the most dynamic elements in the M.I.C.E. segment. The industry is generally regulated under the tourism sector.

In the technical sense, a **convention** is a meeting of delegates or representatives. The 1947 Newfoundland National Convention is a classic example of a state-sponsored political convention. More often, organizations made up of smaller units, chapters, or lodges, such as labor unions, honorary societies, and fraternities and sororities, meet as a whole in convention by sending delegates of the units to deliberate on the organization's common issues. This also applies to a political convention, though in modern times the common issues are limited to selecting a party candidate or party chairman. In this technical sense, a congress, when it consists of representatives, is a convention. The British House of Commons is a convention, as are most other houses of a modern representative legislature. The National Convention or just "Convention" in France comprised the constitutional and legislative assembly which sat from September 20, 1792 to October 26, 1795.

Many sovereign states have provisions for conventions besides their permanent legislature. The Constitution of the United States of America has a provision for the calling of a constitutional convention, whereby delegates of the states are summoned to a special meeting to amend or draft the constitution. This process has never occurred, save for the original drafting of the constitution, although it almost happened in several cases. The US Constitution also has provisions for constitutional amendments to be approved by state conventions of the people. This occurred to ratify the original constitution and to adopt the twenty-first amendment, which ended prohibition. *Con* is a common abbreviation for convention, and some conventions (such as DEF CON and Gen Con) use it in their names.

Trade Show & Convention Selling

When you participate in a trade show, many types of people with different objectives will attend your booth. One of the most challenging aspects of running an exhibit and making sales afterwards involves the qualification of prospects. Measuring the likelihood that a random lead will result in a purchase is important because your sales team does not have an infinite amount of time to do their job. Your sales people have a limited amount of time to follow up on leads and wasting their day on a dead-end lead will squander your company's money.

The most important rule when qualifying prospects is to NEVER ignore anyone who comes to your booth. Even if someone looks like they aren't in the market to buy, you should still be polite and helpful. Someone who doesn't need your services may know a friend or colleague who does. However, you cannot afford to spend all day talking to people who are never going to make a purchase. Determining if your visitors are trying to educate themselves, make a purchase, or simply wander around, will help you to save time. Remember that it does not matter how big or popular a visitor's company is. A small business owner may buy a $30,000 display, while a Fortune 500 company representative may be looking for a cheap pop-up for their next event.

The best way to determine the quality of leads is to simply ask questions. The following questions will help you figure out who will be a legitimate source of revenue and who will drain your resources. You should ask:

1. What do you like and what would you change about your current supplier?
2. How do our products compare to the products of your current supplier?
3. What information do you need to make a good decision?
4. What are your main objectives and goals for your event?
5. What is your primary concern when making a purchase?
6. What are some challenges you have experienced lately?
7. How do you decide which suppliers to work with?
8. What specific products or services do you need?
9. What do you think should be the next step?

Answers to these questions will not necessarily qualify a prospect, but you can gain an understanding of their current situation, mood and buying behavior based on their responses. Remember that people do not like to be drilled with questions, so try to be subtle when gathering all of this information.

Aside from these questions, you should also analyze your prospect to determine the final decision maker, their budget (don't ask directly, but feel it out), their timeline for making a decision, and if they are working with a competitor of yours. You can also make some valuable assumptions about a visitor's intentions by analyzing their tone of voice, level of interest, and body language. Use all of this information to make a reasonable decision about whether or not to focus your efforts on a visitor at your booth.

Sometimes, you can let your leads do the work for you. Set up an online form with a few short questions. You could also hand out hard copy forms at your event. The form could contain questions about what problems they are experiencing, what they think they need, how soon they need it, their primary decision criteria, and issues with current suppliers. You can then analyze their answers to determine if they are a genuine lead worth targeting. However, if those people even take the time to fill out a questionnaire, they are probably worth a serious follow up.

They may be difficult to spot, but investigative competitors may show up to your booth and you should be polite to them. However, do not waste more time than necessary; remember your true audience.

Although the environment is unique, gathering leads at trade shows, conventions and events is an extremely valuable use of time. Staying focused and accurately qualifying prospects is more important than ever; spend your time wisely and you can return home with a fistful of solid follow-ups.

Brad Collmeyer is a digital marketing consultant currently working with Apple Rock, an industry leading strategic partner in event planning, trade show displays and trade show services. Our creative and comprehensive approach ensures that businesses connect with their audience, whether using a custom trade show booth or through a full-scale experiential marketing campaign designed around their goals. With over two decades of industry experience, and scores of award-winning custom trade show displays and visual marketing creations, Apple Rock is the premier event planning and trade show company with the creative edge and the strategic mindset to transform the mundane into the extraordinary.

Language, Structure and Content of the CISG

The CISG is written using 'plain language that refers to things and events for which there are words of common content'. This was a conscious intent to allow national legal systems to be transcended through the use of a common legal *lingua franca* and avoids the 'words associated with specific domestic legal nuances'. Further, it facilitated the translation into six languages so all texts are equally authentic.

The CISG is divided into four parts:-

Part I - Sphere of Application and General Provisions (Articles 1-13)

The CISG applies to contracts of sale of goods between parties whose places of business are in different States when these States are Contracting States (Article 1(1) (a)). Given the significant number of Contracting States, this is the usual path to the CISG's applicability.

The CISG also applies if the parties are situated in different countries (which need not be Contracting States) and the conflict of law rules lead to the application of the law of a Contracting State. For example, a contract between a Japanese trader and a Brazilian trader may contain a clause that arbitration will be in Sydney under Australian law with the consequence that the CISG would apply. It should be noted that a number of States have declared they will not be bound by this condition.

The CISG is intended to apply to commercial goods and products only. With some limited exceptions, the CISG does not apply to domestic goods, nor does it apply to auctions, ships, aircraft or intangibles and services. The position of computer software is 'controversial' and will depend upon various conditions and situations.

Importantly, parties to a contract may exclude or vary the application of the CISG.

Interpretation of the CISG is to take account of the 'international character' of the Convention, the need for uniform application and the need for good faith in international trade. Disputes over interpretation of the CISG are to be resolved by applying the 'general principles' of the CISG or where there are no such principles but the matters are governed by the CISG (a gap *praeter legem*) by applying the rules of private international law.

A key point of controversy had to do with whether or not a contract requires a written memorial to be binding. The CISG allows for a sale to be oral or unsigned but in some countries, contracts are not valid unless written. In many nations, however, oral contracts are accepted and those States had no objection to signing, so States with a strict written requirement exercised their ability to exclude those articles relating to oral contracts, enabling them to sign as well.

Part II - Formation of the Contract (Articles 14–24)

An offer to contract must be addressed to a person, be sufficiently definite – that is, describe the goods, quantity and price – and indicate an intention for the offeror to be bound on acceptance. Note that the CISG does not appear to recognise common law unilateral contracts but, subject to clear indication by the offeror, treats any proposal not addressed to a specific person as only an invitation to make an offer. Further, where there is no explicit price or procedure to implicitly determine price then the parties are assumed to have agreed upon a price based upon that 'generally charged at the time of the conclusion of the contract for such goods sold under comparable circumstances'.

Generally, an offer may be revoked provided the withdrawal reaches the offeree before or at the same time as the offer or before the offeree has sent an acceptance. Some offers may not be revoked, for example when the offeree reasonably relied upon the offer as being irrevocable.

The CISG requires a positive act to indicate acceptance; silence or inactivity are not an acceptance.

The CISG attempts to resolve the common situation where an offeree's reply to an offer accepts the original offer but attempts to change the conditions. The CISG says that any change to the original conditions is a rejection of the offer – it is a counter-offer – unless the modified terms do not materially alter the terms of the offer. Changes to price, payment, quality, quantity, delivery, liability of the parties and arbitration conditions may all materially alter the terms of the offer.

Part III - Sale of Goods (Articles 25–88)

Articles 25 – 88; sale of goods, obligations of the seller, obligations of the buyer, passing of risk, obligations common to both buyer and seller.

The CISG defines the duty of the seller, 'stating the obvious', as the seller must deliver the goods, hand over any documents relating to them and transfer the property in the goods, as required by the contract. Similarly, the duty of the buyer is to take all steps 'which could reasonably be expected' to take delivery of the goods, and to pay for them.

Generally, the goods must be of the quality, quantity and description required by the contract, be suitably packaged and fit for purpose. The seller is obliged to deliver goods that are not subject to claims from a third party for infringement of industrial or intellectual property rights in the State where the goods are to be sold. The buyer is obliged to promptly examine the goods and, subject to some qualifications, must advise the seller of any lack of conformity within 'a reasonable time' and no later than within two years of receipt.

The CISG describes when the risk passes from the seller to the buyer but it has been observed that in practice most contracts define the 'seller's delivery obligations quite precisely by adopting an established shipment term' such as FOB and CIF.

Remedies of the buyer and seller depend upon the character of a breach of the contract. If the breach is fundamental then the other party is substantially deprived of what it expected to receive under the contract. Provided that an objective test shows that the breach could not have been foreseen , then the contract may be avoided and the aggrieved party may claim damages. Where part performance of a contract has occurred then the performing party may recover any payment made or good supplied ; this contrasts with the common law where there is generally no right to recover a good supplied unless title has been retained or damages are inadequate, only a right to claim the value of the good.

If the breach is not fundamental then the contract is not avoided and remedies may be sought including claiming damages, specific performance and adjustment of price. Damages that may be awarded conform to the common law rules in *Hadley v Baxendale* but it has been argued the test of foreseeability is substantially broader and consequently more generous to the aggrieved party.

The CISG excuses a party from liability to a claim of damages where a failure to perform is attributable to an impediment beyond the party's, or a third party sub-contractor's, control that could not have been reasonably expected. Such an extraneous event might elsewhere be referred to as force majeure, and frustration of the contract.

Where a seller has to refund the price paid then the seller must also pay interest to the buyer from the date of payment. It has been said the interest rate is based on rates current in the seller's State 'since the obligation to pay interest partakes of the seller's obligation to make restitution and not of the buyer's right to claim damages' , although this has been debated. In a mirror of the seller's obligations, where a buyer has to return goods the buyer is accountable for any benefits received.

Part IV - Final Provisions (Articles 89-101)

Articles 89 – 101; final provisions including how and when the Convention comes into force, permitted reservations and declarations, and the application of the Convention to international sales where both States concerned have the same or similar law on the subject.

The Part IV Articles, along with the Preamble, are sometime characterized as being addressed 'primarily to States' , not to business people attempting to use the Convention for international trade. They may, however, have a significant impact upon the CISG's practical applicability, thus requiring careful scrutiny when determining each particular case.

Commentary Upon the Convention

Although the Convention has been accepted by a large number of States, it has been the subject of some criticism. For example, the drafting nations have been accused of being incapable of agreement on a code that 'concisely and clearly states universal principles of sales law' and through the Convention's invitation to interpret taking regard of the Convention's 'international character' gives judges the opportunity to develop 'diverse meaning'. Put more bluntly, the CISG has been described as 'a variety of vague standards and compromises that appear inconsistent with commercial interests'.

A contrary view is that the CISG is 'written in plain business language' which allows judges the opportunity to make the Convention workable in a range of sales situations. It has been said 'the drafting style is lucid and the wording simple and uncluttered by complicated subordinating clauses', and the 'general sense' can be grasped on the first reading without the need to be a sales expert.

Uniform application of the CISG is problematic because of the reluctance of courts to use 'solutions adopted on the same point by courts in other countries' , resulting in inconsistent decisions. For example, in a case involving the export to Germany by a Swiss company of New Zealand mussels with a level of cadmium in excess of German standards, the German Supreme Court found that it is *not* the duty of the seller to ensure that goods meet German public health regulations. This contrasted with a later decision in which an Italian cheese exporter failed to meet French packaging regulations and the French court decided it is the duty of the seller to ensure compliance with French regulations.

These two cases were held by one commentator to be an example of contradictory jurisprudence. While another commentator saw the cases as not contradictory as the German case could be distinguished on a number of points. It is noticeable that the French court chose not to consider the German court's decision in its published decision. In any event, it would seem that if there is room for contrary decisions on the obligation for a seller to conform to the regulations in force in the buyer's State and the exceptions to that obligation then the Convention should be clarified to increase certainty, particularly if the reluctance to use foreign precedent continues.

CISG advocates are also concerned that the natural inclination of judges is to interpret the CISG using the methods familiar to them from their own State rather than attempting to apply the general principles of the Convention or the rules of private international law. This is despite the comment from one highly respected academic that 'it should be a rare, or non-existent, case where there are no relevant general principles to which a court might have recourse' under the

CISG. This concern has been supported by research of the CISG Advisory Council which has said, in the context of the interpretation of Articles 38 and 39, there is a tendency for courts to interpret the articles in the light of their own State's law and some States have 'struggled to apply appropriately'. In one of a number of criticisms of Canadian court decisions to use local legislation to interpret the CISG one commentator said the CISG was designed to 'replace existing domestic laws and case law' and attempts to resolve gaps should not be by 'reference to relevant provisions of sales law'.

Critics of the multiple language versions of the CISG claim it is inevitable the versions will not be totally consistent because of translation errors and the untranslatability of 'subtle nuances' of language. This argument, although with some validity, would not seem peculiar to the CISG but common to any and all treaties that exist in multiple languages. The *reductio ad absurdum* would seem to be that all international treaties should exist in only a single language, something which is clearly neither practical nor desirable.

Other criticisms of the Convention are that it is incomplete, there is no mechanism for updating the provisions and no international panel to resolve interpretation issues. For example, the CISG does not govern the validity of the contract, nor does it consider electronic contracts.

Despite the critics, a supporter has said 'the fact that the costly ignorance of the early days, when many lawyers ignored the CISG entirely, has been replaced by too much enthusiasm that leads to ... oversimplification, cannot be blamed on the CISG'.

Future Directions

Greater acceptance of the CISG will come from three directions. Firstly, it is likely that within the global legal profession, as the numbers of new lawyers educated in the CISG increases, the existing Contracting States will embrace the CISG, appropriately interpret the articles and demonstrate a greater willingness to accept precedents from other Contracting States.

Secondly, business people will increasingly pressure both lawyers and governments to make sales of goods disputes less expensive and reduce the risk of being forced to use a legal system that may be completely alien to their own. Both of these objectives can be achieved through use of the CISG.

Finally, UNCITRAL will need to develop a mechanism to further develop the Convention and to resolve conflicting interpretation issues. This will make it more attractive to both business people and potential Contracting States.

Differences with Country Legislation Relating to the Sale of Goods

Depending on the country, the CISG can represent a small or significant departure from local legislation relating to the sale of goods, and in this can provide important benefits to companies from one contracting state that import goods into other states that have ratified the CISG.

Many countries that have signed the CISG have made declarations and reservations as to the Treaty's scope.

Differences with Legislation in the United States of America

In the USA, 49 of 50 states have adopted common legislation referred to in the U.S. as the Uniform Commercial Code ("UCC"). The UCC is similar to the CISG in most ways as a means for promoting contracts for the sales of goods. The UCC departs from the CISG in some areas, such as the following areas that tend to reflect more general aspects of the U.S. legal system:

Terms of Acceptance - Under the CISG, acceptance occurs when it is received by the offeror, a rule similar to many civil law jurisdictions which contemplate for service to be effective upon receipt; by contrast the U.S. legal system often applies the so-called "mailbox" rule by which, acceptance, like service, can occur at the time the offeree transmits it to the offeror.

"Battle of Forms" - Under the CISG, a reply to an offer that purports to be an acceptance, but has additions, limitations, or other modifications is generally considered by the CISG to be a rejection and counteroffer. The UCC, on the other hand, tries to avoid the "battle of forms" that can result from such a rule, and allows an expression of acceptance to be operative, unless the acceptance states that it is conditioned on the offeror consenting to the additional or different terms contained in the acceptance.

Writing Requirement - Unless otherwise specified by a ratifying state, the CISG does not require that a sales contract be reduced to a writing. Under the UCC's statute of frauds, oral contracts selling goods for a price of $500.00 or more are generally not enforceable unless in writing.

Nevertheless, because the U.S. has ratified the CISG, it has the force of federal law and supersedes UCC-based state law under the Supremacy Clause. Among the U.S. reservations to the CISG is the provision that the CISG will apply only as to contracts with parties located in other CISG Contracting States, a reservation permitted by the CISG in Article 95. Therefore, in *international* contracts for the sale of goods between a U.S. entity and an entity of a Contracting State the CISG will apply unless the contract's choice of law clause specifically provides for non-CISG terms, or for the application of the law of a non-Contracting State.

Conversely, in "international" contracts for the sale of goods between a U.S. entity and an entity of a non-Contracting State, to be adjudicated by a U.S. court, the CISG will not apply and the contract will be governed by the domestic law applicable according to private international law rules.

Convention Service

Convention services were brought under the Service Tax net by the Finance Act, 2001, w.e.f. 16th July, 2001 vide Notification No. 4/2001, dated 9-7-2001. The services shall be taxed if provided by any commercial concern for holding formal meeting or assembly not open to the general public.

Rate of Service Tax: The rate of service tax is specified in section 66 of the Act. The Finance (No. 2) Act, 2004 has substituted the charging section 66, and the rate of service tax is enhanced from 8% to 10% ad valorem. The increase in tax rate has come into force from the date of enactment of the Finance (No. 2) Act, 2004 Le. 10-9-2004. Further, the Finance (No. 2) Act, 2004, w.e.f. 10-9-2004 has also levied an education cess @ 2 % of the service tax. The cess paid on inputs services shall be available as credit for payment of cess on output services. For further discussion in this regard, refer to -'Payment of Service Tax'.

Convention Services

The definition of convention service has been given under clause (32) of section 65. It provides:

"Convention means a formal meeting or assembly which is not open to the general public, but does not include a meeting or assembly, the principal purpose of which is to provide any type of amusement, entertainment or recreation".

Therefore, the services which fall under the category of convention are

1. Formal meeting or assembly, which is not open to the general public; but
2. It does not include a meeting or assembly the principal purpose of which is to provide any type of amusement, entertainment or recreation.

(1) 'Formal'

The term 'formal' means 'according to form or established mode' (reference the Chambers English Dictionary) or 'conforming to accepted rules or custom' (reference the Oxford Mini Dictionary).

(2) 'Meeting' or 'Assembly'

The term 'meeting' or 'assembly' is interchangeable. That means 'an organized assembly for transaction of business' (reference the Chambers English Dictionary) or 'coming together' (reference the Oxford Mini Dictionary).

(3) 'General Public'

As per the definition of the convention, it does not include the meeting or assembly that is open to the general public. In other words, only private meeting or assembly, where general public cannot participate falls under the service tax net. The words 'general public' in the present context mean where the participation is not restrictive to any particular segment of the society or group or organization but open for all. Therefore, any programmes like musical concert, cultural programme, cinema or other sports event, etc. which are open for the general public would be out of the ambit of convention for the purpose of present context of service tax.

(4) 'Principal Purpose of Amusement'

As per the definition of the convention, it does not include a meeting or assembly the principal purpose of which is to provide any type of amusement, entertainment or recreation. The 'principal' here means the main object. The terms 'amusement', 'entertainment' or 'recreation' have not been specifically defined in the context of service tax. Therefore, these terms should be understood in the context of its commonly understood meaning and scope. Therefore, when family members, friends and relatives together organize any party to celebrate birthday party or new year's eve, or marriage anniversary, etc. the 'meeting' or 'assembly' is to be treated the principal purpose of which is amusement, entertainment or recreation and strictly would be out of the ambit of convention services. But, it may be noted that they are falling under the 'mandap keeper's services', therefore, service tax may be charged for such social function under such category of services.

(5) Providing Facilities for Convention is Also Convention

Yes, the Government in, its Circular F. No. B. 11/1/2001-TRU, dated 9th July, 2001 (appended in Annexure 1) has clarified that the convention services, apart from providing space for holding a convention, could also include providing other facilities such as video conferencing, equipment such as overhead projectors, video-room (LCD projector), speakers, microphones, technical staff for operating these equipments and stationery, etc. for holding a convention.

Therefore, formal meeting or assembly means organizing people in a group to transact any business according to accepted rules or custom. Therefore, person must assemble at a place where such business shall be transacted. However, it has been clarified by the Government that even providing facilities for holding of convention will also come under the service tax net, therefore, it would not be necessary that meeting must be at a place but it may be in 'any manner' like through video conferencing. Further, in the definition of convention, it has been provided that such meeting or assembly should not be open to the general public as well. It also does not include a meeting or assembly principal purpose of which is to provide any type of amusement, entertainment or recreation. Therefore, in the present context of service tax, holding of convention includes any service provided for holding a conference, seminar, meetings, etc. like 'annual general meeting of the company,' meeting of board of directors, meeting of doctors or other professionals.

(6) Convention Services are Same as Mandap Keeper Services

The Government in its Circular F. No. B. 11/1/2001-TRU, dated 9th July, 2001 (appended as Annexure 1) has clarified that in some cases it may appear that convention services is same as the service rendered by a "mandap keeper". There is a subtle distinction between the types of events such as official, social or business function in the case of mandap keeper as opposed to formal meeting in the case of convention services. However, the Finance Act, 2003, w.e.f. 14-52003, has introduced a new section 65A to provide the manner of determination of classification of taxable services, which has been discussed in detail in the - 'Classification of Services'. Therefore, now, determination of classification of taxable service shall be made according to the manner given in the provision of Section 65A and tax shall be paid according to that category of taxable service.

(7) Convention Services are also Charged as Mandap Keeper Services or Vice Versa

No, the Government in its Circular F. No. B. 11/1/2001-TRU, dated 9th July, 2001 (appended as Annexure 1) has clarified that the intention is not to charge the service tax twice on the same service. If a service provider is already registered as a mandap keeper and paying service tax, he is not liable to pay service tax again under the category of convention services. Similarly, a convention service is also not liable to tax as mandap keeper service. As mentioned earlier in the Finance Act, 2003, w.e.f. 14-5-2003, has introduced a new section 65A to provide the manner of determination of classification of taxable services. Therefore, now, determination of classification of taxable service shall be made according to the manner given in the provision of Section 65A and tax shall be paid according to that category of taxable service. Thus, the clarification given in the aforesaid Circular will become redundant, as the classification of services have become necessary and strictly in accordance with the manner provided in the section 65, for more details, refers to - 'Classification of Services'.

(8) Holding of Convention by Chambers of Commerce and Industries are Covered Under the Service Tax

In a point raised before the Government - whether holding of conventions by Chambers of Commerce and Industry for their members would be liable to service tax? the Government has clarified that service tax, in the case of convention services, is applicable only when the service is provided by a commercial concern. If the Chamber of Commerce and Industry is not a commercial concern, then the tax does not apply. The memorandum and articles of association of a Chamber of Commerce and Industry would indicate whether it is a commercial concern or not. It is informed by the Chambers that generally they are not commercial concerns. Therefore, holding of conventions by Chambers of Commerce and Industry for their members would not attract service tax.

Taxable Service

The definition of taxable service provided by any commercial concern has been given under sub-clause (zc) of clause (105) of section 65. That is: 'any service provided "to a client, by any commercial concern in relation to holding of convention, in any manner".

LIABLE TO PAY SERVICE TAX

Service tax is liable to be paid when convention services are rendered by any commercial concern.

(1) 'Commercial Concern'

The term 'commercial concern' denotes a firm or a business entity or organization, engaged in commercial activities like sale, purchase or providing services for consideration and having profit motive. A charitable institution cannot fall under the category of a 'commercial concern', because it does not have profit motive. The term 'commercial concern' in the context of service tax means the concern engaged in providing services of holding of convention.

Therefore, service tax is liable to be paid only when convention services are rendered by any 'commercial concern' engaged in business of rendering service relating to holding of convention.

Convention Services Liable to be Charged to Tax

Convention services liable to be charged when provided to

1. A client;
2. In any manner.

(1) Client—Services are liable to be charged to tax only when it is provided to a 'client'. The word 'client' as per the dictionary meaning means "a person who employs a lawyer or professional adviser: a customer" (reference the Chambers English Dictionary) or "a person using the services of a professional person; customer" (reference the Oxford Mini Dictionary).

Therefore, the 'client' is necessarily an external person who hires or uses the services of another person for consideration. Service tax will attract only if services are rendered to a client, not to the other department within the same concern. In other words, services must be provided to the separate entity or external person. When services are provided to the charitable institution for which no fee is charged it is not a client. Therefore, there is no question of service tax unless services are provided to a client on payment basis.

(2) Meaning of 'in any manner'—Services are subject to tax when provided 'in any manner'. The words 'in any manner' signifies 'directly or indirectly'. Thus, facilitation activities, such as video conferencing, equipment like overhead projectors, video-room (LCD projector), speakers, microphones, technical staff for operating these equipments and stationery, etc. for holding a convention are taxable.

Sometimes, it may be possible that service provider may not alone be able to execute the work and take the help of other person or concern by employing them on sub-contract basis for the execution of work. In other words, services may be rendered by the commercial concern through help or assistance of other commercial concern. In this case, even if service provider get a part of the service done by employing the services of other person or concern, it will be treated that services are provided by the original service provider and tax would be charged on the entire services.

The Value of Taxable Services for Charging Tax

The value of taxable services in relation to convention services provided by any commercial concern to the client shall be the gross amount charged from the client in relation to holding formal meeting or assembly.

When any commercial concern provides facilitation activities such as video conferencing, equipments like overhead projectors, video-room (LCD projector), speakers, etc. for holding a convention, the service charges paid for the use of these facilities also form part of taxable value.

Explanation 1 has also been added to section 67, which provides, for the removal of doubt, in respect of only certain specific services, it is declared that certain amount shall form part of value of taxable services and certain amount shall not form part of the value of taxable services, but nothing has been specified in respect of convention services.

(1) Charges for Providing Facilities for Convention are Part of Taxable Value—Yes, the Government in its Circular F. No. B. 11/1/2001-TRU, dated 9th July, 2001 (appended as Annexure 1) has clarified that the convention services,. apart from providing space for holding a convention, could also include providing other facilities such as video conferencing, equipment such as overhead projectors, video-room (LCD projector), speakers, microphones, technical staff for operating these equipments and stationery, etc. The charges for such facilities shall also be included in the value of taxable service.

Therefore, in case of convention services, the value of taxable services shall be the gross amount charged by the service provider for such services rendered by him without claiming any abatements towards administrative/ office expenses incurred for rendering such services. In other words, 'gross amount' here indicate that no deduction shall be allowed in respect of any expenditure incurred by the service provider which has proximate connection in rendering the services by him.

(2) Abatement From Value of Taxable Services—The Government, w.e.f. 9-7-2004, has provided an abatement of 40% of 'the gross amount charged from a client by any commercial concern for computation of service tax in relation to holding a convention. However, such exemption/ abatement shall be available when convention service is provided including catering service. In other words, in this case, service tax would be leviable on 60% of the gross amount charged for convention services [vide Notification No. 10/2004-ST, dated 9-7-2004 (appended as Annexure II)]. The Government has provided aforesaid exemption at par with exemption provided to Hotels under 'mandap keeper service', whereas hotels were provided exemption/ abatement (w.e.f. 20-12-2001) for providing 'mandap keeper service' provided food is also supplied but such benefit of abatement was not extended for providing convention services. The above exemption has removed the said anomalies. However, it may be noted that abatement under 'mandap keeper service' is available only to Hotels whereas abatement under convention services is available irrespective of the fact that service is rendered by Hotels or by any other commercial concern. The aforesaid Notification has been amended w.e.f. 10-9-2004, vide Notification No. 12/2004-ST, dated 10-9-2004, and now the abatement under the aforesaid Notification shall be available if no credit of duty paid on inputs or capital goods has been taken under the provisions of the CENVAT Credit Rules, 2004 (which has been discussed in the 'Credit of service tax and excise duty'). Further, now the abatement under the aforesaid Notification shall not be available if such commercial concern in relation to holding a convention has availed the benefit under Notification No. 12/2003 Service Tax, dated 20th June, 2003 (which has been discussed in the 'Payment of Service Tax').

Exempted Services

The Government has granted exemption from the whole of Service Tax in respect of all taxable services, for services provided to United Nations or an International Organisation. Similarly, the exemption, subject to certain conditions, has also been granted for taxable service provided to a developer or units of Special Economic Zone (SEZ). The Government, w.e.f. 20 November, 2003 has restored the exemption, as an interim measure, from the whole of service tax when payment is received in convertible foreign exchange for the taxable services rendered in India provided it was not repatriated from or sent outside India, such exemption was earlier withdrawn w.e.f. 1-3-2003. The reader may note that detailed discussion about aforesaid exemptions along with relevant notifications have been given in the 'Exemption from whole of Service Tax - Some Cases'.

N.B. The readers may note that provisions, procedures and other related discussion related to registration, payments of service tax, filing of return, interest and penalty, assessment procedure, appeal, refund of tax, etc., which are same, as applicable in respect of other taxable services, have been given.

Hague Service Convention

The Convention on the Service Abroad of Judicial and Extrajudicial Documents in Civil or Commercial Matters, more commonly called the Hague Service Convention, is a multilateral treaty which was signed in The Hague on 15 November 1965 by members of the Hague Conference on Private International Law. It allows service of judicial documents from one signatory state to another without use of consular and diplomatic channels. The issue of international service had been previously addressed as part of the 1905 Civil Procedure Convention which was also signed in The Hague. The 1905 convention however did not command wide support and was ratified by only 22 countries.

Prior to the enactment of the Hague Service Convention, service of process in civil cases was generally effected by a *letter rogatory*, a formal request from the court in the country where proceedings were initiated or underway to a court in another country where the defendant resided. This procedure generally required transmission of the document to be served from the originating court to the foreign ministry in the state of origin. The foreign ministry in the state of origin forwarded the request to the foreign ministry in the destination state. The foreign ministry would then forward the documents to the local court where the party to be served resided and the local court would arrange for service on the party to be served. Once service was made, a certificate of service (proving that service was made) would then pass through the same channels in reverse. Under a somewhat more streamlined procedure, courts could sometimes forward service requests to the foreign ministry or the foreign court directly, cutting out one or more steps in the process. To affect service in states which have not ratified the Hague Service Convention, parties often still have to follow this cumbersome and time-consuming procedure.

The Hague Service Convention established a more simplified means for parties in signatory states to affect service in other signatory states. Under the Convention, each contracting state is required to designate a "Central Authority" to accept incoming requests for service. A "Judicial Officer" who is competent to serve process in the state of origin is permitted to send request for service directly to the "Central Authority" of the state where service is to be made. Upon receiving the request, the "Central

Authority" in the receiving state arranges for service in a manner permitted within the receiving state, typically through a local court to the defendant's residence. Once service is affected, the "Central Authority" sends a certificate of service to the "Judicial Officer' who made the request. Parties are required to use three standardized forms: (1) a request for service, (2) a summary of the proceedings (similar to a summons), and (3) a certificate of service. The main benefits of the Hague Service Convention over Letters Rogatory is that it is faster (requests generally take 2 - 4 months rather than 6 - 12 months), it uses standardized forms which should be recognized by authorities in signatory countries, and in most cases, it is cheaper because service can be affected by the local attorney without hiring a foreign attorney to advise on how to serve.

The Hague Service Convention does not prohibit a receiving state from permitting international service by other methods otherwise authorized by local law (for example, service directly by mail or personal service by a person otherwise authorized to service process in the foreign country). For example, in the United States, service can often be made by a private process server. States which permit parties to use these "alternative means" of service make a separate designation in the documents they file with the Convention.

Country-by-country Issues

In the United States, an attorney is usually regarded as an officer of the court. The question arises whether an attorney is therefore a judicial officer, who can send a service request directly to the central authority in another country, within the meaning of the convention. As a practical matter, that depends on the interpretation of the particular central authority. Some countries, such as Israel, only honor a service request by a judge or clerk of the requesting court.

The interpretation of a provision in article 10(a) in controversial. The provision permits the requesting judicial officer to "send" judicial documents by postal channels to countries that authorize this usage in ratifying the convention, such as France and Italy. Other provisions of the convention say "serve" or "service". The controversy is over whether the provision permits service directly on parties by mail. In the United States, some courts interpret this provision to permit service by mailing documents directly to individuals; others hold that the provision only authorizes sending, but not serving, documents by mail. The European Court of Justice and courts in Greece and Alberta interpret the provision to permit formal service by mail. Other countries, including Germany, Switzerland, and most current and former communist countries, require incoming service to be effected exclusively through the country's central authority.

An opinion of the United States Supreme Court said, although only in *dicta*, that wherever the Hague Service Convention applies, use of its procedures are mandatory, in lieu of other means of serving judicial documents. *Volkswagenwerk Aktiengesellschaft v. Schlunk*, 486 U.S. 694, 699 (1986).

In legal practice the reality is different; the "judging court" is master to decide if service abroad was "acceptable" (long arm), and article 10 refers to how each country will serve from their local jurisdiction request coming from abroad and can not impose foreign jurisdictions how to serve (i.e. serving a national abroad). Some central authorities accept service completed by attorneys at law who will serve a foreign request directly without the central authority intervention and the central authority will even issue an affidavit of service for this private personal service. In conclusion any court anywhere can name a "Spacial Process Server", giving him the mandate to serve, subrogating jurisdictional powers as far as this foreign process servers complies with local laws of civil procedure.

Convention Sale Manager

A DMO convention sales manager is responsible for marketing a destination to groups for conferences/meetings, special events, sports/teams and group sales. The convention sales manager works closely with area hotels, venues, facilities and community leaders to prepare bid proposals for selected meetings or events. A successful sales manager is service-oriented, highly motivated and organized.

Job responsibilities may require the sales manager to:

1. Market the DMO within assigned market segments.
2. Take a leadership role in working with local hotel and venue partners in selling the assets of the DMO.
3. Plan and attend industry tradeshows, sales blitzes and events with travel partners.
4. Coordinate details of meetings, such as solicitation of vendors, program development, housing coordination, event layout, menu planning, decoration, event set-up, purchasing, pre-registration, check-in and event tracking.
5. Establish and maintain positive relationships with area hotels, venues, local officials and regional, national and international organizations and associations.
6. Prepare comprehensive bid proposals, as required by potential customers.
7. Stay up-to-date on industry best practices, standards and benchmarks by reading publications and attending continuing education classes.

8. Develop qualified sales leads for the hotels, and track the status of those leads.
9. Make personal bid presentations to meeting planners, as required.
10. Conduct site inspections of venues with planners who represent definite potential for business.
11. Work closely with the communications department to ensure proper press coverage and visibility for secured business when appropriate.
12. Assist in the development of marketing brochures and collateral sales material.

Training, Other Qualifications, and Advancement

On average, a convention sales manager has at least two years of progressive sales experience within the hospitality, meetings or events field. In addition to work experience, most DMOs require an associate's degree, and some require a bachelor's degree. A job applicant must possess a proven track record of excellent communication and leadership skills, along with a high level of initiative. Demonstrated sales success in the hospitality industry and a working knowledge of computer systems and related software applications are preferred. Ability to travel and availability to work evenings and weekends are required.

Earnings

Based on the Destination Marketing Association International's 2008 Compensation & Benefits Survey, the average base compensation for a convention sales manager is $48,550, and the average total compensation is $53,790. Total compensation represents the sum of fixed salary, performance-based cash compensation and transaction-based cash compensation. All figures are averages (means).

Group/Convention Sales Manager

Convention sales can substantially increase business in casino hotels during slow periods at the facilities. In order to keep rooms filled, casino hotels often market their facilities to conventions, conferences, and other groups. Many hotels have constructed their own private convention facilities. Some areas hosting gaming also have centrally located major convention centers. As a result, casino hotels have become important convention destinations. The Convention or Group Sales Manager is responsible for seeking out groups looking for locations to hold their meetings. The hotel often sells rooms at a reduced price to these groups because they are buying blocks of rooms. In addition to selling rooms, the Sales Manager offers groups food and beverage service for meetings and banquets, meeting rooms, ballrooms, and convention facilities.

The Sales Manager is Responsible for Maintaining Established Accounts

He or she must also look for new business by contacting representatives of government, business, or social groups to solicit convention or conference business for the casino hotel. The individual is responsible for analyzing the requirements of the group. He or she will then develop a proposal outlining the services and quoting prices the casino hotel can offer. The Sales Manager is responsible for developing marketing packages, telemarketing, and direct mail promotions to attract new group business. The individual may work with others in advertising, marketing, and public relations on these projects. The individual works closely with other departments to make sure groups that are booked receive proper service. Once a group is booked, the Sales Manager alerts the convention services manager about the contract to assure that groups' needs are taken care of and that they are satisfied with their visit. The Group or Convention Sales Manager may be required to go on the road on occasion to make contact with groups, to meet important clients, and to attend trade shows and sales meetings. The Sales Manager makes calls to prospective clients or has sales packages sent to potential clients. The individual works with hotel sales representatives in closing deals. Other duties of a Casino Hotel Convention or Group Sales Manager may include:

1. Conducting training seminars and workshops for salespeople
2. Assigning leads to salespeople
3. Drawing up contracts and obtaining required signatures

Group/Convention Sales Managers working in casino hotels earn between $50,000 and $95,000 or more annually.

People in some casinos may earn bonuses or commissions on business brought into the hotel or business over and above that which has been forecast. Factors affecting earnings include the geographic location, size, and prestige of the specific casino or casino hotel, as well as the experience, responsibilities, and professional reputation of the individual.

Employment prospects for talented Group Sales Managers are good. Casino hotels, like others in the hospitality industry, are always on the lookout for people who can produce.

The Greatest Number of Opportunities Can be Found in Las Vegas

Countless casino hotels and new mega resorts are being built. Other good opportunities can be found in Reno, Laughlin, Lake Tahoe, Atlantic City, Biloxi, Baton Rouge,

New Orleans, and Detroit. Other regions hosting Indian gaming and land-based or riverboat gaming facilities offer additional job possibilities. Group/Convention Sales Managers may advance their careers by locating similar positions in larger, more prestigious casino hotels. Some individuals may be promoted to the position of director of sales if the facility has such a job. Depending on the career aspirations and training of the individual, he or she may also move into the marketing department. A bachelor's degree is usually required or preferred by most casino hotels for Group or Convention Sales Managers. In some settings, work experience may be accepted in lieu of formal education. Good choices for majors include marketing, sales, public relations, communications, or hotel management and administration.

Group/Convention Sales Managers need experience in hotel sales, group or convention sales, or tours and travel. Some people also have held similar positions with hotels not involved in the gaming industry prior to being employed at a casino hotel. Sales Managers should be personable, pleasantly aggressive people with sales ability. Communication skills are necessary. Individuals should be organized and detail-oriented. The ability to negotiate is mandatory. Those interested in learning more about careers as Group/Convention Sales Managers may obtain additional information from the American Hotel and Lodging Association (AH&LA).

Start with Sales

1. Casinos often promote from within. If you have sales ability, start as a sales representative and work your way up the career ladder.
2. Send, fax, or visit the human resources departments of casino hotels to inquire about job openings. You

might also consider sending or faxing a résumé and a short cover letter.

3. Jobs may be advertised in the classified sections of newspapers in areas hosting gaming. Look under classifications such as "Casino/Gaming Opportunities," "Convention Sales Manager," "Group Sales Manager," "Hotel Sales," or "Casinos/Casino Hotels."
4. Openings are often advertised on the Internet. They may be located via the home pages of casino hotels. They may also be found by doing a search of "Casino," "Casino Hotel," or "Gaming Job Opportunities."

2

Promoting Hospitality Properties

Hospitality is the relationship between guest and host, or the act or practice of being hospitable. Specifically, this includes the reception and entertainment of guests, visitors, or strangers, resorts, membership clubs, conventions, attractions, special events, and other services for travelers and tourists. The word *hospitality* derives from the Latin *hospes,* which is formed from *hostis,* which originally meant "to have power." The meaning of "host" can be literally read as "lord of strangers." *Hostire* means "equalize or compensate."

The contemporary West, hospitality is rarely a matter of protection and survival, and is more associated with etiquette and entertainment. However, it still involves showing respect for one's guests, providing for their needs, and treating them as equals. Cultures and subcultures vary in the extent to which one is expected to show hospitality to strangers, as opposed to personal friends or members of one's in-group.

The hospitality service industry includes hotels, casinos, and resorts, which offer comfort and guidance to strangers, but only as part of a business relationship. The terms hospital, hospice, and hostel also derive from "hospitality," and these institutions preserve more of the connotation of personal care. Hospitality ethics is a discipline that studies this usage of hospitality.

Global Concepts

Pakhtuns

The Pakhtun people of South-Central Asia, predominant in the Khyber Pakhtunkhwa province of Pakistan and Afghanistan have a strong code of hospitality. They are a people characterized by their use of *Pakhtunwali*, an ancient set of ethics, the first principle of which is *Milmastiya* or Hospitality. The general area of Pakhtunistan is also nicknamed *The Land of Hospitality*.

Biblical and Middle Eastern

In Middle Eastern Culture, it was considered a cultural norm to take care of the strangers and foreigners living among you. These norms are reflected in many Biblical commands and examples.

The obligations of both host and guest are stern. The bond is formed by eating salt under the roof, and is so strict that an Arab story tells of a thief who tasted something to see if it was sugar, and on realizing it was salt, put back all that he had taken and left.

Classical World

To the ancient Greeks and Romans, hospitality was a divine right. The host was expected to make sure the needs of his guests were seen to. The ancient Greek term *xenia*, or *theoxenia* when a god was involved, expressed this ritualized guest-friendship relation.

Celtic Cultures

Celtic societies also valued the concept of hospitality, especially in terms of protection. A host who granted a person's request for refuge was expected not only to provide food and shelter to his/her guest, but to make sure they did not come to harm while under their care.

India

In India, hospitality is based on the principle *Atithi Devo Bhava*, meaning "the guest is God." This principle is shown in a number of stories where a guest is literally a god who rewards the provider of hospitality. From this stems the Indian approach of graciousness towards guests at home, and in all social situations.\

Backpacking

Backpacking is a term that has historically been used to denote a form of low-cost, independent international travel. Terms such as independent travel and/or budget travel are often used interchangeably with backpacking. The factors that traditionally differentiate backpacking from other forms of tourism include but are not limited to the following: use of public transport as a means of travel, preference of youth hostels to traditional hotels, length of the trip vs. conventional vacations, use of a backpack, an interest in meeting the locals as well as seeing the sights.

The definition of a backpacker has evolved as travelers from different cultures and regions participate and will continue to do so, preventing an air-tight definition. Recent research has found that, "...backpackers constituted a heterogeneous group with respect to the diversity of rationales and meanings attached to their travel experiences. ...They also displayed a common commitment to a non-institutionalised form of travel, which was central to their self-identification as backpackers." Backpacking as a lifestyle and as a business has grown considerably in the 2000s as the commonplace of low-cost airlines, hostels or budget accommodation in many parts of the world, and digital communication and resources make planning, executing, and continuing a long-term backpacking trip easier than ever before.

While there is no definitive answer as to the precise origin of backpacking, its roots can be traced, at least partially, to the Hippie trail of the 1960s and 70s, which in turn followed sections of the old Silk Road. In fact, some backpackers today seek to re-create that journey, albeit in a more comfortable manner, while capitalizing on the current popularity of the green movement. Looking further into history, Giovanni Francesco Gemelli Careri has been cited by some as one of the world's first backpackers.

While travel along the old Hippie Trail has been rendered complicated since the early 80s due to unrest in Afghanistan, Iraq and Iran that continues today, backpacking has expanded to most regions of the world. In recent years, the increase of budget airlines and low-cost flights has contributed to this expansion. At present, new "hippie trails" are being formed towards Northern Africa in places such as Morocco and Tunisia and other destinations being reached by low-cost airlines.

Technological changes and improvements have also contributed to changes in backpacking. Traditionally backpackers did not travel with expensive electronic equipment such as laptop computers, digital cameras and PDAs due to concerns about theft, damage, and additional luggage weight. However, the desire to stay connected coupled with trends in lightweight electronics have given rise to the flashpacking trend, which has been in a state of continuous evolution in recent years. Simultaneous with a change in "what" they're carrying, backpacking is also becoming less and less reliant on the physical backpack in its initial form although the backpack can still be considered the primary luggage of backpackers.

Culture

Of importance in backpacking is a sense of authenticity. Backpacking is perceived as being more than a vacation, but a means of education. Backpackers want to experience the "real" destination rather than the packaged version often associated with mass tourism, which has led to the assertion that backpackers are anti-tourist. There is also the feeling of "sneaking backstage" and witnessing real life with more involvement with local people.

Criticism

Backpacking, like other forms of travel, remains controversial. Some of these criticisms date back to travelers' actions along the Hippie Trail. Criticism comes from many sides, including the host countries and other travelers who disagree with the actions of backpackers although the perception of backpackers seems to have improved as backpacking has become more mainstream. Erik Cohen notes that even though one of the primary aims of backpacking is to seek the authentic, the majority of backpackers spend most of their time interacting with other backpackers and interactions with locals are of "secondary importance".

Couch Surfing

Couch Surfing is a hospitality exchange network and website. With almost 2.5 million members in 245 countries and territories, CouchSurfing has an Alexa Traffic Rank of about 2,500. Couchsurfing is a neologism referring to the practice of moving from one friend's house to another, sleeping in whatever spare space is available, floor or couch, generally staying a few days before moving on to the next house.

Membership

Free to register, members have the option of providing information and pictures of themselves and of the sleeping accommodation they offer, if any. More information provided by a member, and other members, improves the chances that someone will find the member trustworthy enough to be his host or guest. Security is often measured in the reference established by networking. Volunteers may verify names and addresses. Members looking for accommodation can search for hosts using several parameters such as age, location, gender and activity level.

Homestays are consensual between the host and guest, and the duration, nature, and terms of the guest's stay are generally worked out in advance. No monetary exchange takes place except for compensation of incurred expenses (e.g. food).

CouchSurfing provides editable travel guides and forums where members may seek travel partners or advice. CouchSurfing's main focus is "social networking" and members organise activities such as camping trips, bar crawls, meetings, and sporting events.

The website features a searchable database of hundreds of upcoming events organised by CouchSurfing members, including the annual "Berlin Beach Camp" which draws over 1,000 attendees, the annual "WinterCamp," and a New Year's Eve party hosted in a different city in Europe every year. Famous Couchsurfers include Julian Assange and Daniel Bedingfield.

Security Verification

There are three methods designed to increase security and trust, which are all visible on member profiles for potential hosts and surfers:

1. Personal references, which hosts and surfers have the option to leave after having used the service.
2. An optional credit card verification system, allowing members to "lock in" their name and address by making a credit card payment and entering a code that CouchSurfing mails to an address of their choice. This also allows CouchSurfing to recoup some costs by requiring a fee for verification. For fairness, the verification fee is based on a sliding scale, taking into account the Purchasing Power Parity and Human Development Index of the country of residence.
3. A personal vouching system, whereby a member that had been vouched for three times — originally starting with the founders of the site — might in turn vouch for any number of other members he knew or had met through CouchSurfing, and trusts.

Ambassadors

Members who wished to volunteer for various tasks on the site and help spread the word about CouchSurfing in general were able to become ambassadors. Ambassadors must be role-models and actively promote the CouchSurfing spirit among members and to the public. In addition to promoting use of the site, they greet new members, help with questions and perform other administrative tasks, all on a volunteer basis. No new ambassadors are being created at this time.

Demographics

As of January 2011, there were over 2.4 million persons who were registered with Couchsurfing, a population comparable in size to Latvia or Jamaica.

As of January 2011, couchsurfers represents more than 80,000 unique towns in 245 states and territories. Around 20% of the couchsurfers had registered their country as being the United States, with Germany, France, Canada and England also registering large numbers of participants. The city with the largest number of resident couchsurfers was Paris.

English was spoken by nearly 74% of registered Couchsurfers. French (20%), Spanish (17%) and German (16%) were also spoken. The average age of participants was 28 years of age.

History

The CouchSurfing project was conceived by Casey Fenton in 1999. According to Fenton's account, the idea arose after finding an inexpensive flight from Boston to Iceland. Fenton randomly e-mailed 1,500 students from the University of Iceland asking if he could stay. He ultimately received more than 50 offers of accommodation. On the return flight to Boston, he began to develop the ideas that would underpin the CouchSurfing project.

Fenton developed the code intermittently over the next few years. The site was launched with the cooperation of Dan Hoffer, Sebastien Le Tuan, and Leonardo Silveira as a beta in January 2003. The project became a public website in January 2004.

Initial growth of the site was slow. By the end of 2004 the site had just over 6,000 members. In 2005, growth accelerated and by the end of the year, membership stood at just under 45,000. As of 29 January 2011, CouchSurfing have almost 2.5 million members and is the most popular free accommodation site. The site has an Alexa Traffic Rank of 2,584.

2006 Database Loss and Relaunch

In June 2006, the project experienced a number of computer problems resulting in much of the database being irrevocably lost. Due to the volume of critical data that had been lost, Casey Fenton was of the opinion that the project could not be resurrected. On 29 June 2006, he sent an e-mail to all members: "It is with a heavy heart that I face the truth of this situation. CouchSurfing as we knew it doesn't exist anymore."

Fenton's e-mail was met with vocal opposition to the termination of the project and considerable support for its recreation. A CouchSurfing Collective was underway in Montreal at the time and those in attendance committed to fully recreating the original site, with users to re-enter their profile data. "CouchSurfing 2.0" was announced early in July 2006, with the intent to be operational within 10 days. The initial implementation of CouchSurfing 2.0 actually launched after only four days with the current CouchSurfing slogan *"Participate in Creating a Better World, One Couch At A Time"*. Since the site relaunch, the project has received international media coverage.

2009 Leeds Incident

On 5 March 2009 in Leeds, UK, a man named Abdelali Nachet raped a woman from Hong Kong who stayed at his place through the CouchSurfing project. Nachet was sentenced to 10 years in prison.

Organization

Mission

The mission statement of CouchSurfing is *Create Inspiring Experiences*: "At CouchSurfing International, we envision a world where everyone can explore and create meaningful connections with the people and places they encounter. Building meaningful connections across cultures enables us to respond to diversity with curiosity, appreciation and respect. The appreciation of diversity spreads tolerance and creates a global community."

Couch Surfing Collectives

Since June 2006, development of the website has been run in large part by CouchSurfing Collectives: events which may last days or weeks, bringing groups of CouchSurfers together in a chosen city, to develop and improve CouchSurfing. Previous Collectives took place in Montreal, Vienna, New Zealand, Rotterdam, Thailand, Alaska, Costa Rica and Istanbul.

Tax Status

CouchSurfing International Inc. is a non-profit corporation incorporated in the U.S. state of New Hampshire. An application for the federal 501(c)(3) non-profit status was filed in November 2007. As of January 1 2011 CouchSurfing is not in the "list of organizations eligible to receive tax-deductible charitable contributions". This means that its non-profit status is in question.

Hospitality Club

The Hospitality Club is an international, Internet-based hospitality service of appr. 647,000 members in 226 countries Its members use the website HospitalityClub.org to coordinate accommodation and other services, such as guiding or regaling travelers. Hospitality Club is currently the second largest such hospitality network. Hospitality Club was founded by Veit Kühne in 2000 with the help of friends and family as a general-purpose Internet-based hospitality exchange organization. The organization, open to anybody, followed from a similar network organized by Veit Kühne exclusively for members of the student exchange organization AFS. The concept for Hospitality Club was inspired by the SIGHT hospitality network of Mensa and it is the successor of Hospex, the first Internet based hospitality exchange network, established in 1992 and with which it joined forces in 2005. Membership has since increased dramatically.

Functioning

Membership in the organization is free and is obtained simply by registering on the website. The core activity of the organization is exchange of accommodation. Acting as a host, a member offers the possibility of accommodation at his leisure. As a guest, a traveler may find possible hosts and contact them through the website. No money is involved — guests and hosts do not pay each other. The duration of the stay, whether food is provided for free, for a fee or not at all, and all other conditions are agreed on beforehand to the convenience of both parties.

After meeting, the host and guest may comment about each other. This provides a means to establish reputation which is the main security measure. Users have to provide their real identity, which is screened by volunteers, and protected against changes. Apart from accommodation, members exchange other forms of hospitality, such as guiding visitors or providing travel-related advice. There are also wiki-like *Travel Guide* sections and forums where members may seek partners for travels, hitchhiking etc.

Volunteers within the club often arrange meetings or camps which are events that last several days that bring people together.

Organization and Policies

The club is based on the work of hundreds of volunteers around the world. The motivation behind it is *the idea that bringing people together and fostering international friendships will increase inter cultural understanding and strengthen peace.* It is one of the largest hospitality networks, and there is *a mission to find 1,000,000 friendly people.*

The policy of the club explicitly forbids alternative uses, such as dating, job-seeking, commercial use, and website promotions. In order to protect members' mailboxes from spam and to keep trust in the network at high levels a volunteer team scans the messages being sent across the site. Members may also opt-out of this service and receive all messages directly.

Hospitality Service

The concept of hospitality exchange, also known as "accommodation sharing", "hospitality services" (short "hospex"), and "home stay networks", refers to centrally organized social networks of individuals, generally travelers, who offer or seek accommodation without monetary exchange. These services generally connect users via the internet. In 1949, Bob Luitweiler founded the first hospitality service called Servas Open Doors as a cross national, non-profit, volunteer run organization advocating interracial and international peace. In 1965, John Wilcock set up the Traveler's Directory as a listing of his friends willing to host each other when traveling. In 1988, Joy Lily rescued the organization from imminent shutdown, forming Hospitality Exchange. In 1970 Jimmy Carter (then US

President) announced the formation of Friendship Force International which has chapters in 57 countries today. In 2000, Veit Kuhne founded Hospitality Club, the first Internet-based service. In 2004, Casey Fenton started CouchSurfing, now the largest hospitality exchange organization.

How they Work

Generally, after registering, members have the option of providing very detailed information and pictures of themselves and of the sleeping accommodation being offered, if any. The more information provided by a member improves the chances that someone will find the member trustworthy enough to be their host or guest. Names and addresses may be verified by volunteers. Members looking for accommodation can search for hosts using several parameters such as age, location, sex, and activity level. Home stays are entirely consensual between the host and guest, and the duration, nature, and terms of the guest's stay are generally worked out in advance to the convenience of both parties. No monetary exchange takes place except under certain circumstances (e.g. the guest may compensate the host for food). After using the service, members can leave a noticeable reference about their host or guest.

Instead of or in addition to accommodation, members also offer to provide guide services or travel-related advice. The websites of the networks also provide editable travel guides and forums where members may seek travel partners or advice. Many such organizations are also focused on "social networking" and members organize activities such as camping trips, bar crawls, meetings, and sporting events.

Some networks cater to specific niche markets such as students, activists, religious pilgrims, and even occupational groups like police officers.

Benefits

Monetary Savings

As these networks provide accommodation at no charge, monetary savings can be significant.

Local Contact

Hospitality exchange gives travelers the chance to experience what life is like for people living in other places. In addition, making interpersonal connections and fostering understanding of different cultures may in the long run also be important to international relations. During hospitality exchanges, hosts may show off their local knowledge and exciting places "off the tourist map". Not only may travelers get a distinct experience, but they will also get a feel for the everyday lives of local residents.

Reciprocity

The concept behind Hospitality services is based on the pay it forward philosophy, gift economy, and reciprocal altruism.

Drawbacks

Lack of Guarantee

There is no contractual agreement between users in these systems. Reservations are made, but if they are for some reason broken, there is no higher authority to which one could plead for a refund or other compensation. The only repercussion will be the poor rating you give that user and your only consolation will be that your warning will deter others from visiting or hosting them. For those who feel insecure unless their travel arrangements are written in stone before departure, this system will not be comforting.

Potential Interpersonal Conflict or Awkwardness

There is a chance that guest and host will not get along. Perhaps there will be scheduling or ideological conflicts. Maybe you will find that hosts or visitors have misrepresented themselves. Perhaps the experience will not live up to your expectations. Intense interpersonal communications in advance and a flexibility once you have arrived is your best bet. These experiences require additional planning and courtesy towards the demands of your host. Thus, your living conditions, length of stay, and overall experience will be circumscribed by the living conditions you enter into.

Digital Divide and Demographic Segregation

As use of these services generally requires access to the internet and knowledge of the English language, the sample population found in searches of these databases is really much less diverse than a geographical representation of worldwide users might suggest.

Security

Staying in someone's house, or inviting people into your house leaves open the possibility of being taken advantage of.

Example Networks

There are countless websites that serve the idea of hospitality service, with new ones appearing as this phenomenon becomes more popular. While this page is not intended to be a directory listing, here is a small sample of the well-established and long-standing networks:

1. CouchSurfing - A very active network with over 2 million members in more than 200 countries

2. Friendship Force International A network of chapters worldwide which concentrates on building understanding across cultures.
3. Hospitality Club - A very active network with over 550,000 members in more than 200 countries
4. Servas International - human rights and global peace oriented since 1949. A relatively small network now with over 15,000 members(?) with a very long history.
5. Tripping - A global network of travelers with the motto "For Travelers, Not Tourists"
6. BeWelcome

Specialized Networks

Some networks offer specialised hospitality services.

1. Lesbian and Gay Hospitality Exchange International
2. Warm Showers - Hospitality network for touring cyclists
3. Dachgeber - Hospitality network for touring cyclists in Germany with about 3000 members
4. Pasporta Servo - for Esperanto speakers
5. WWOOF - "Worldwide Opportunities on Organic Farms", help on the property is exchanged for food, accommodation, education and cultural interaction
6. Freagle - "Free Camping, worldwide!" - Uniting Outdoor Lovers Through Hospitality and Mutual Help.
7. HelpX - "Help Exchange", help is exchanged for food, accommodation, experience and cultural interaction
8. Homeshare International - charitable organization providing exchange of housing for help in the home
9. Ridester - ride sharing for travelers in USA

Hospitality Management Studies

Hospitality management is the academic study of the hospitality industry. A degree in Hospitality management is often conferred from either a university college dedicated to the studies of hospitality management or a business school with a department in hospitality management studies. Degrees in hospitality management may also be referred to as hotel management, hotel and tourism management, or hotel administration. Degrees conferred in this academic field include Bachelors of Arts, Bachelors of Business Administration, Bachelors of Science, Masters of Science, MBA, and Doctorate of Philosophy. Hospitality management studies provides a focus on management of hospitality operations including hotels, restaurants, cruise ships, amusement parks, destination marketing organizations, convention centers, country clubs, and related industries.

Curriculum

In America, Hospitality and Tourism Management curriculum follow similar core subject applications to that of a business degree but with a focus on hospitality management. Core subject areas include accounting, administration, finance, information systems, marketing, human resource management, public relations, strategy, quantitative methods, and sectoral studies in the various areas of hospitality business. Cornell University, University of Nevada, Las Vegas (UNLV), and University of Central Florida (UCF) are considered the top Hospitality Management undergraduate colleges in America. One of the newest graduate degree programs in hospitality management is offered by The George Washington University School of Business in Washington, D.C..

In addition to the core coursework above, degree-specific coursework normally includes:

1. Restaurant Management (Examples: Management of Food and Beverage Operations, Food Science, Food Selection and Preparation, Food and Beverage Cost Control)
2. Lodging Operations (Examples: Lodging Management, Hotel Operations, Resort Timeshare Management, Reservation Sales and Marketing, Hospitality Physical Plant)
3. Global Tourism (Examples: Tourism Management, Airline Industry, Sustainable Tourism, Hospitality and Research Methods)
4. Attractions Management (Examples: Theme Park Management, Entertainment Arts)
5. Event Management (Examples: Event Industry, Catering Management, Hospitality Marketing Management)
6. Food Preparation (Examples: Basic Food Preparation, Food Sanitation, Beer and Wine Labs)

Many hospitality programs require concurrent field experience within the industry in the form of internships or co-operative placements.

Graduate Placement

Several large hospitality corporations such as Marriott, Hilton Worldwide, IHG, Hyatt, Sasi park, Wyndham, beeran international Parks and Resorts, and various management companies offer internship programs as well as management training programs and direct placements for students majoring in Hospitality and Tourism Management. Similar to other business fields, management training programs and direct placement opportunities are highly competitive.

Hospitality Management in The Netherlands

Tio University (in Utrecht) provides the Hotel and Event management study in English and Dutch.

Hospitality Management in The Stellenbosch South Africa

1. The management techniques and practices of the hospitality industry in the United States are viewed as the best in the world. AHA South Africa's academic programmess are designed to meet the growing needs of the hospitality industry by placing equal emphasis on attitude and aptitude. Students graduate with AHA's IHMS' world-class Diploma in International Hospitality Management (DIHM).

The aim of the DIHM Programme is to offer students, who wish to begin working at the supervisory level within the industry, a comprehensive hospitality management education. Students will be introduced to all aspects of hospitality services operations, and the wide array of career opportunities available within the industry.

Upon successful completion of the DIHM Programme, it is expected that graduates will have developed:

1. The technical and supervisory management skills and product knowledge necessary for a career in the hospitality industry.
2. The ability to think logically and communicate clearly.
3. An inter-disciplinary approach to problem-solving and decision-making.
4. A global perspective on the operations of the industry.

Course Curriculum

Semester One Code Title HM 101 Introduction to Hospitality and Tourism SOC 101 Service Basics SOC 102

Cultural Diversity COM 101 Language of Hospitality COM 102 Computer Applications FB 101 Food and Beverage Service CA 101 Introduction to Culinary Arts CA 102 Health and Food Safety FB 103 Cape Wine Academy Prelim Course WBL Work Based Learning (30 Hours)

Semester Two Code Title COM 103 Business Communication FB 102 Revenue and Menu Management FB104 Food and Beverage Management FB 105 Wines of the World HM 103 Event Planning HM 104 Inventory and Purchasing HM105 Hospitality Accounting CA 103 Quantity Food Production CA 104 Nutrition WBL Work Based Learning (30 hours)

Semester Three Code Title COM 105 Business Entrepreneurship SOC 103 Leadership Development HM 106 Front Office Operations HM 107 Lodging Management HM 108 Sales and Marketing HM 109 Human Resource Management WBL Work Based Learning (120 hours)

Semester Four Code Title HM 111 Local Internship

SEMESTER FIVE AND SIX Code Title HM 112 International Internship (Optional) CODE DESCRIPTION HM Hospitality Management CA Culinary Arts SOC Social Sciences COM Communication FB Food and Beverage

Grading System

Guest Swimming Pool and Dining Tables at The Private Hotel School. We understand that students learn in many different ways and we do our best to broaden the means by which we assess them accordingly. Students will be assessed on class participation in discussions, assignments, discussion of articles, and practical applications with components of each complete module and other activities as well as through the more traditional means of quizzes and examinations.

Attendance is important and is a part of the final assessment. Participation is also highly valued, as we strive to produce graduates who have a good work ethic, strive for excellence, are willing to go the extra mile in their future careers and come to work with a positive, willing-to-do-whatever-it-takes approach. We therefore reward the development of those values in class participation.

Grading Scale

Performance of students will be rated at the end of each semester in accordance with the following grading system. GradeDenotes Percent Range % A+ = Outstanding 96 - 100 A = Excellent 91 - 95 B+ = Very Good 86 - 90 B = Good 81 - 85 C+ = Satisfactory 76 - 80 C = Pass 70 - 75 F = Fail 0 - 69 INC = Incomplete

We apply continuous assessment at the Private Hotel School. Students are therefore assessed on their performance during the semester as well as an examination at the end of the semester.

Passing Grade

Students must receive a grade of "C" (minimum 70%) to pass in each subject. A student who incurs a grade of "F" in any course, is required to retake the course and obtain a passing grade. Any financial implications of retaking a course will be at a cost of R4600.

Attendance

The PHS aims to prepare students to be successful professionals. Attendance and punctuality are important work ethics for students to develop. An attendance of at least 80% in all theoretical classes and 90% of all practical classes is required. The total of excused absences should therefore not exceed 20% of theoretical course hours and

10% of practical course hours. Students who are absent, whether excused or unexcused, in more than the indicated requirements, are considered to have officially withdrawn from that course and will be given a grade of "F" in that course.

Hotel Addiction to OTAs

There are many things in life that, when used in moderation, are fun and even good for you. Chocolate, wine and sex are good examples. However, when taken to excess they can become addictive and hazardous to your physical and financial health. The same holds true in hospitality...

Online travel agencies (OTAs) are a valuable marketing and third-party distribution resource for hotels. Used in moderation they can provide a base level of occupancy, a steady stream of revenue and help during seasonal troughs. However, when taken to excess, OTAs can be hazardous to the financial health of your hotel.

Consider the following facts:

1. OTA Share Increasing—2009 and 2010 were not banner years for the travel industry causing hotels to rely more heavily on third parties. According to online consultant Phocuswright, share of sales on hotel websites fell dramatically as they continued to divert more inventory – and sales – to OTAs.

Phocuswright also points out, "OTA and hotel websites attract different types of customers – OTAs draw budget-conscious consumers while hotel websites lure more frequent, higher spending travelers."

2. Maximizing RevPAR—An extensive study of more than 10,000 hotels by STR Analytics concludes, "the more properties dropped rates, the worse their RevPAR index change was, indicating that the upside in occupancy performance did not compensate for the sacrifice in rate."

3. A Billion Here, a Billion There—According to a Hospitality eBusiness Solutions (HeBS) analysis, "hotels stand to lose a staggering $5.4 billion in revenue leakage through third party sites in 2010." *A billion here, a billion there and pretty soon you're talking about real money!*

Many hoteliers are becoming addicted to OTAs – dumping inventory and waiting for large checks without stopping to calculate the hidden cost of commissions, which are deducted before payment to the hotels. Hidden commissions that hotels pay to OTAs (the leakage) are a marketing expense.

This is money that could be used to market directly to potential guests to get them to book direct.

3 Steps to Breaking this Addiction Cycle

If your hotel is receiving a considerable portion of guests through OTAs, here are three steps you need to take now:

1. Identify Your Hidden Costs—There's probably no line item for "OTA Commissions" in your budget. So you can't simply run a report to get actual costs. That's why we created a special Hotel-OTA Hidden Cost Calculator. How much is your hotel spending?

In the example above, this relatively small 75-room resort is getting one-third of its business from OTAs. The cost? More than $400,000!That's probably more than the hotel's total marketing budget, which supports the other two-thirds of its business including direct (a much more profitable source).How much is your property contributing to the estimated $5.4 billion that hotels are sending to the OTAs? How addicted is your hotel?

2. Determine Your Ideal Sales Mix - Now that you know your hidden costs, it's time to reclaim this money and put it to better use. To do that, you need to decide what the ideal mix of direct and indirect business should be for your hotel and establish targets. What will be your mix for the next six months? One year? Two years? You get the picture.

Use the Hidden Cost Calculator to play out several "what if" scenarios. What if the hotel in the example above could keep everything the same, but reduce OTAs as a percentage of total revenue from 33% to 20%? They would reduce their annual OTAs spending to $244,664, saving close to $160,000 annually.

Some of the anticipated savings will need to be reinvested in marketing to build more profitable direct business. And herein lays the dilemma. Can you afford to invest in the direct channel before you begin to realize any savings? The answer is yes, but only if you employ the right strategies. The earlier you start the easier and more profitable it will be. As with any addiction, the longer you wait, the more dependent you become and the harder it is to break the cycle.

3. Refocus on Direct to Consumer Marketing – Now that you know what percentage of your business OTAs *should* represent, it's time to reorient your marketing. If you are going to invest in direct to consumer marketing, there is only one rule to remember – invest where there are proven results and a positive return on investment (ROI).

There are a slew of marketing approaches, but the one that continues to provide consistently outstanding performances is Customer Relationship Marketing or CRM. We have seen CRM:

1. Increase a profitable luxury hotel's direct business from 25% to more than 65%.
2. Assist another small luxury hotel in avoiding OTAs altogether. It now maintains its destination's highest level of occupancy and has 80% direct bookings.

3. Help several hotels minimize rate reductions and recover quickly from recessions.
4. Give hotels control over their destiny as opposed to handing it over to a third party.

CRM is a discipline designed to both acquire and retain profitable guests. Its roots are in the science of direct and database marketing. It may appear similar to traditional advertising, but is a very different way to approach customers, nurture relationships and build direct sales.

CRM is bigger than the Internet. It integrates all of the marketing disciplines, including the Internet, direct marketing, advertising, public relations and promotion into one cohesive communications program. The program is designed to move individuals along the customer lifecycle, from building awareness through creating a loyal, profitable repeat guest.

The foundation of CRM is a database, which is fed by all marketing activities and is constantly updated, segmented and fine tuned to reach guests and prospects on a one-to-one basis with targeted messages. Communicating one-to-one and encouraging dialogue builds relationships and loyal guests.

Beginning the Path to Recovery with CRM

Well, it's not a simple process. If it were, every hotel would be doing it. The rewards, however, far exceed the cost for hoteliers looking and willing to refocus their marketing approach. As with any recovery, it's one day at a time. CRM is a gradual process, where your hotel gets stronger with increased direct business over time. But at some point you need to commit to doing things differently or resign yourself to being happy with the results you're currently receiving.

Here are a few things to get started:

1. Make sure your Internet strategy is in order. Your website needs to be up-to-date, easy to navigate, search engine optimized and have a user-friendly booking engine. How does your site compare to your competitors? Analyze your web stats and make adjustments as needed.
2. Build and maintain a high quality database of prospects and guests. Do you have a newsletter sign-up on your website? Be sure to capture personal data, which you can use to segment individuals to deliver relevant information.
3. Ban the "blast" mentality. You don't like being blasted with mass emails and neither does anyone in your database. If your agency wants to send an "email blast," it's a sure sign they are clueless about direct marketing, one-to-one marketing or CRM.
4. Critique your messages. Are you sending informative, creative and engaging news about your hotel and destination (and a special or two) that nurtures a relationship and keeps your hotel top of mind? Or are you blasting people with special sales hoping to find someone in the mood to book? Being relevant is much more effective at building immediate and long term sales, and brand equity.
5. Keep the relationship going. Think of CRM as building customer relationships before, during and after a stay. Most hotels, particularly small luxury hotels, pride themselves on taking excellent care of guests on property. That same care must be taken in all marketing messages to nurture each relationship. CRM keeps the focus on customers in a closed loop process, not on "transactional" stays.

6. Don't ignore travel agents. Use the same direct marketing techniques to build relationships with travel agents. They can be a productive source of business and a more favorable commission rate than the OTAs.

CRM can help dramatically increase your share of direct bookings, build more loyal customers and make your hotel more profitable.

Advertising Comes to TripAdvisor

In "How Important is Word of Mouth Advertising" Nielsen Internet Research was presented showing that consumers around the world place their highest levels of trust in other consumers. Their #1 trusted source? Friends and relatives as always. The #3 trusted source (a fraction behind Newspapers) was online reviews written by people readers didn't even know!

TripAdvisor just joined forces with Facebook to bring Online Word of Mouth Advertising to a brand new level. As TripAdvisor is now advertising, Facebook fans can now "plan the best trip of your life with the help of friends." And 50% of all TripAdvisor members are on Facebook.

Some of the online innovations seen so far this year include:

1. TripAdvisor announced a mobile app so millions of smartphone users can access hotel reviews wherever they may be.
2. Google announced Place Search allowing web searchers to get a profile of various hotels without ever visiting a hotel's web site. TripAdvisor reviews play a big role in how your hotel's Google Place Search profile.
3. TripAdvisor announced and recently upgraded its app for the iPAD.

4. And now TripAdvisor and Facebook have joined forces.

TripAdvisor is no longer just a hotel review web site. It is one of the most important and influential travel planning sources on the Internet today.

What's really fascinating is the power of this marketing behemoth can be put to use by your hotel for practically nothing. A business listing certainly won't break the bank.

After that, the only two things needed to ensure positive TripAdvsior reviews is a good customer experience and a some coordinated hotel manpower. Here's what you have to do:

1. Have a well thought out TripAdvisor review strategy
2. Put someone in charge of implementing it
3. Regularly review to monitor performance
4. Adjust the strategy as necessary to make sure it works. Demand that it works!

With your hotel's reputation on the line and the power of online and offline Word of Mouth advertising at stake, this sure seems like one of the best marketing investments any hotel can make.

Hospitality Industry Consultants Specializing in the Hotel Marketing Strategies

DB&A consults regularly for owners, lenders, operators and managers advising clients with recommendations, ideas and opinions on specific ways of improving overall hospitality sales and marketing performance and measurement. Brudney's research skills produce helpful tools for management in assessing competition, overall hotel market conditions, primary and secondary feeder markets along with invaluable hotel user feedback.

Making Plans... Not Promises

David Brudney & Associates produces hands on actionable hotel marketing plans and, in order for owners and management to make certain that dollars are being spent wisely and that staff is meeting expectations, DB&A performs annual and quarterly reviews and evaluations of entire sales and marketing plan and operation.

Put DB&A's Hotel Marketing Expertise to Work for You! As a veteran professional consultant, company principle, David Brudney has advised developers and lenders, hotel owners and operators, chains and independents, mega-resorts and conference centers, limited service and B&Bs alike, throughout the U.S. on issues relating to performance evaluation and enhancement, hotel marketing strategies, structure, direction and execution.

DB&A's area of expertise is sales, marketing and operations and his primary hospitality consulting work the past 28 years has focused on producing top line improvement, strategic planning, structure and direction, performance evaluation, result measurement, research and litigation support.

Customized Hospitality Marketing Consulting Services:

1. Hotel Sales & Marketing operation performance, production, metrics, planning, direction and deployment benchmarking and validation
2. Implementation, monitoring; and results measurement Mentoring
3. Speaking, facilitating, training
4. Dispute resolution, litigation support, expert witness.

3

Use of Computer Technology in Convention Sales and Service

A computer is a programmable machine designed to sequentially and automatically carry out a sequence of arithmetic or logical operations. The particular sequence of operations can be changed readily, allowing the computer to solve more than one kind of problem. Conventionally a computer consists of some form of memory for data storage, at least one element that carries out arithmetic and logic operations, and a sequencing and control element that can change the order of operations based on the information that is stored. Peripheral devices allow information to be entered from external source, and allow the results of operations to be sent out.

A computer's processing unit executes series of instructions that make it read, manipulate and then store data. Conditional instructions change the sequence of instructions as a function of the current state of the machine or its environment. The first electronic computers were developed in the mid-20th century (1940–1945). Originally, they were the size of a large room, consuming as much power as several hundred modern personal computers (PCs).

Modern computers based on integrated circuits are millions to billions of times more capable than the early machines, and occupy a fraction of the space. Simple computers are small enough to fit into mobile devices, and can be powered by a small battery. Personal computers in their various forms are icons of the Information Age and are what most people think of as "computers". However, the embedded computers found in many devices from MP3 players to fighter aircraft and from toys to industrial robots are the most numerous.

History of Computing

The history of computing hardware is the record of the ongoing effort to make computer hardware faster, cheaper, and capable of storing more data. Computing hardware evolved from machines that needed separate manual action to perform each arithmetic operation, to punched card machines, and then to stored-program computers. The history of stored-program computers relates first to computer architecture, that is, the organization of the units to perform input and output, to store data and to operate as an integrated mechanism. Secondly, this is a history of the electronic components and mechanical devices that comprise these units. Finally, we describe the continuing integration of 21st-century supercomputers, networks, personal devices, and integrated computers/communicators into many aspects of today's society. Increases in speed and memory capacity, and decreases in cost and size in relation to compute power, are major features of the history. As all computers rely on digital storage, and tend to be limited by the size and speed of memory, the history of computer data storage is tied to the development of computers.

Before the development of the general-purpose computer, most calculations were done by humans. Tools to help humans calculate were then called "calculating machines", by proprietary names, or even as they are now, calculators. It was those humans who used the machines who were then called computers; there are pictures of enormous rooms filled with desks at which computers (often young women) used their machines to jointly perform calculations, as for instance, aerodynamic ones required for in aircraft design.

Calculators have continued to develop, but computers add the critical element of conditional response and larger memory, allowing automation of both numerical calculation and in general, automation of many symbol-manipulation tasks. Computer technology has undergone profound changes every decade since the 1940s.

Computing hardware has become a platform for uses other than mere computation, such as process automation, electronic communications, equipment control, entertainment, education, etc. Each field in turn has imposed its own requirements on the hardware, which has evolved in response to those requirements, such as the role of the touch screen to create a more intuitive and natural user interface.

Aside from written numerals, the first aids to computation were purely mechanical devices which required the operator to set up the initial values of an elementary arithmetic operation, then manipulate the device through manual manipulations to obtain the result. A sophisticated (and comparatively recent) example is the slide rule in which numbers are represented as lengths on a logarithmic scale and computation is performed by setting a cursor and aligning sliding scales, thus adding those lengths. Numbers could be represented in a continuous "analog" form, for instance a voltage or some other physical property was set to be proportional to the number. Analog computers, like those designed and built by Vannevar Bush before World War II were of this type. Or, numbers could be represented in the form of digits, automatically manipulated by a mechanical mechanism. Although this last approach required more complex mechanisms in many cases, it made for greater precision of results.

Both analog and digital mechanical techniques continued to be developed, producing many practical computing machines. Electrical methods rapidly improved the speed and precision of calculating machines, at first by providing motive power for mechanical calculating devices, and later directly as the medium for representation of numbers. Numbers could be represented by voltages or currents and manipulated by linear electronic amplifiers. Or, numbers could be represented as discrete binary or decimal digits, and electrically controlled switches and combinational circuits could perform mathematical operations.

The invention of electronic amplifiers made calculating machines much faster than their mechanical or electromechanical predecessors. Vacuum tube (thermionic valve) amplifiers gave way to solid state transistors, and then rapidly to integrated circuits which continue to improve, placing millions of electrical switches (typically transistors) on a single elaborately manufactured piece of semi-conductor the size of a fingernail. By defeating the tyranny of numbers, integrated circuits made high-speed and low-cost digital computers a widespread commodity.

Earliest true Hardware

Devices have been used to aid computation for thousands of years, mostly using one-to-one correspondence with our fingers. The earliest counting device was probably a form of tally stick. Later record keeping aids throughout the Fertile Crescent included calculi (clay spheres, cones, etc.) which represented counts of items, probably livestock or grains, sealed in containers. The use of counting rods is one example.

The abacus was early used for arithmetic tasks. What we now call the Roman abacus was used in Babylonia as early as 2400 BC. Since then, many other forms of reckoning boards or tables have been invented. In a medieval European counting house, a checkered cloth would be placed on a table, and markers moved around on it according to certain rules, as an aid to calculating sums of money.

Several analog computers were constructed in ancient and medieval times to perform astronomical calculations. These include the Antikythera mechanism and the astrolabe from ancient Greece (c. 150–100 BC), which are generally regarded as the earliest known mechanical analog computers. Other early versions of mechanical devices used to perform one or another type of calculations include the planisphere and other mechanical computing devices invented by Abû Rayhân al-Bîrûnî (c. AD 1000); the equatorium and universal latitude-independent astrolabe by Abû Ishâq Ibrâhîm al-Zarqâlî (c. AD 1015); the astronomical analog computers of other medieval Muslim astronomers and engineers; and the astronomical clock tower of Su Song (c. AD 1090) during the Song Dynasty.

The "castle clock", an astronomical clock invented by Al-Jazari in 1206, is thought to be the earliest programmable analog computer. It displayed the zodiac, the solar and lunar orbits, a crescent moon-shaped pointer traveling across a gateway causing automatic doors to open every hour, and five robotic musicians who play music when struck by levers operated by a camshaft attached to a water wheel. The length of day and night could be re-programmed every day in order to account for the changing lengths of day and night throughout the year.

Scottish mathematician and physicist John Napier noted multiplication and division of numbers could be performed by addition and subtraction, respectively, of logarithms of those numbers. While producing the first logarithmic tables Napier needed to perform many multiplications, and it was at this point that he designed Napier's bones, an abacus-like device used for multiplication and division. Since real numbers can be represented as distances or intervals on a line, the slide rule was invented in the 1620s to allow multiplication and division operations to be carried out significantly faster than was previously possible. Slide rules were used by generations of engineers and other mathematically involved professional workers, until the invention of the pocket calculator.

Wilhelm Schickard, a German polymath, designed a calculating clock in 1623, unfortunately a fire destroyed it during its construction in 1624 and Schickard abandoned the project. Two sketches of it were discovered in 1957; too late to have any impact on the development of mechanical calculators.

In 1642, while still a teenager, Blaise Pascal started some pioneering work on calculating machines and after three years of effort and 50 prototypes he invented the mechanical calculator. He built twenty of these machines (called the Pascaline) in the following ten years.

Gottfried Wilhelm von Leibniz invented the Stepped Reckoner and his famous cylinders around 1672 while adding direct multiplication and division to the Pascaline. Leibniz once said "It is unworthy of excellent men to lose hours like slaves in the labour of calculation which could safely be relegated to anyone else if machines were used."

Around 1820, Charles Xavier Thomas created the first successful, mass-produced mechanical calculator, the Thomas Arithmometer, that could add, subtract, multiply, and divide. It was mainly based on Leibniz' work. Mechanical calculators, like the base-ten addiator, the comptometer, the Monroe, the Curta and the Addo-X remained in use until the 1970s. Leibniz also described the binary numeral system, a central ingredient of all modern computers. However, up to the 1940s, many subsequent designs (including Charles Babbage's machines of the 1822 and even ENIAC of 1945) were based on the decimal system; ENIAC's ring counters emulated the operation of the digit wheels of a mechanical adding machine.

In Japan, Ryôichi Yazu patented a mechanical calculator called the Yazu Arithmometer in 1903. It consisted of a single cylinder and 22 gears, and employed the mixed base-2 and base-5 number system familiar to users to the soroban (Japanese abacus). Carry and end of calculation were determined automatically. More than 200 units were sold, mainly to government agencies such as the Ministry of War and agricultural experiment stations.

1801: Punched Card Technology

In 1801, Joseph-Marie Jacquard developed a loom in which the pattern being woven was controlled by punched cards. The series of cards could be changed without changing the mechanical design of the loom. This was a landmark achievement in programmability. His machine was an improvement over similar weaving looms. Punch cards were preceded by punch bands, as in the machine proposed by Basile Bouchon. These bands would inspire information recording for automatic pianos and more recently NC machine-tools.

In 1833, Charles Babbage moved on from developing his difference engine (for navigational calculations) to a general purpose design, the Analytical Engine, which drew directly on Jacquard's punched cards for its program storage. In 1835, Babbage described his analytical engine. It was a general-purpose programmable computer, employing punch cards for input and a steam engine for power, using the positions of gears and shafts to represent numbers. His initial idea was to use punch-cards to control a machine that could calculate and print logarithmic tables with huge precision (a special purpose machine). Babbage's idea soon developed into a general-purpose programmable computer. While his design was sound and the plans were probably correct, or at least debuggable, the project was slowed by various problems including disputes with the chief machinist building parts for it. Babbage was a difficult man to work with and argued with everyone. All the parts for his machine had to be made by hand. Small errors in each item might sometimes sum to cause large discrepancies. In a machine with thousands of parts, which required these parts to be much better than the usual tolerances needed at the time, this was a major problem. The project dissolved in disputes with the artisan who built parts and ended with the decision of the British Government to cease funding. Ada Lovelace, Lord Byron's daughter, translated and added notes to the *"Sketch of the Analytical Engine"* by Federico Luigi, Conte Menabrea. This appears to be the first published description of programming.

A reconstruction of the Difference Engine II, an earlier, more limited design, has been operational since 1991 at the London Science Museum. With a few trivial changes, it works exactly as Babbage designed it and shows that Babbage's design ideas were correct, merely too far ahead of his time. The museum used computer-controlled machine tools to construct the necessary parts, using tolerances a good machinist of the period would have been able to achieve. Babbage's failure to complete the analytical engine can be chiefly attributed to difficulties not only of politics and financing, but also to his desire to develop an increasingly sophisticated computer and to move ahead faster than anyone else could follow.

Following Babbage, although unaware of his earlier work, was Percy Ludgate, an accountant from Dublin, Ireland. He independently designed a programmable mechanical computer, which he described in a work that was published in 1909.

In the late 1880s, the American Herman Hollerith invented data storage on a medium that could then be read by a machine. Prior uses of machine readable media had been for control (automatons such as piano rolls or looms), not data. "After some initial trials with paper tape, he settled on punched cards..." Hollerith came to use punched cards after observing how railroad conductors encoded personal characteristics of each passenger with punches on their tickets. To process these punched cards he invented the tabulator, and the key punch machine. These three inventions were the foundation of the modern information processing industry. His machines used mechanical relays (and solenoids) to increment mechanical counters. Hollerith's method was used in the 1890 United States Census and the completed results were "... finished months ahead of schedule and far under budget". Indeed years faster than the prior census had required. Hollerith's company eventually became the core of IBM. IBM developed punch card technology into a powerful tool for business data-processing and produced an extensive line of unit record equipment. By 1950, the IBM card had become ubiquitous in industry and government. The warning printed on most cards intended for circulation as documents (checks, for example), "Do not fold, spindle or mutilate," became a catch phrase for the post-World War II era.

Leslie Comrie's articles on punched card methods and W.J. Eckert's publication of *Punched Card Methods in Scientific Computation* in 1940, described punch card techniques sufficiently advanced to solve some differential equations or perform multiplication and division using floating point representations, all on punched cards and unit record machines. Those same machines had been used during World War II for cryptographic statistical processing. In the image of the tabulator, note the patch panel, which is visible on the right side of the tabulator. A row of toggle switches is above the patch panel. The Thomas J. Watson Astronomical Computing Bureau, Columbia University performed astronomical calculations representing the state of the art in computing.

Computer programming in the punch card era was centered in the "computer center". Computer users, for example science and engineering students at universities, would submit their programming assignments to their local computer center in the form of a stack of punched cards, one card per program line. They then had to wait for the program to be read in, queued for processing, compiled, and executed. In due course, a printout of any results, marked with the submitter's identification, would be placed in an output tray, typically in the computer center lobby. In many cases these results would be only a series of error messages, requiring yet another edit-punch-compile-run cycle. Punched cards are still used and manufactured to this day, and their distinctive dimensions (and 80-column capacity) can still be recognized in forms, records, and programs around the world. They are the size of American paper currency in Hollerith's time, a choice he made because there was already equipment available to handle bills.

Desktop Calculators

By the 20th century, earlier mechanical calculators, cash registers, accounting machines, and so on were redesigned to use electric motors, with gear position as the representation for the state of a variable. The word "computer" was a job title assigned to people who used these calculators to perform mathematical calculations. By the 1920s Lewis Fry Richardson's interest in weather prediction led him to propose human computers and numerical analysis to model the weather; to this day, the most powerful computers on Earth are needed to adequately model its weather using the Navier-Stokes equations.

Companies like Friden, Marchant Calculator and Monroe made desktop mechanical calculators from the 1930s that could add, subtract, multiply and divide. During the Manhattan project, future Nobel laureate Richard Feynman was the supervisor of the roomful of human computers, many of them female mathematicians, who understood the use of differential equations which were being solved for the war effort.

In 1948, the Curta was introduced. This was a small, portable, mechanical calculator that was about the size of a pepper grinder. Over time, during the 1950s and 1960s a variety of different brands of mechanical calculators appeared on the market. The first all-electronic desktop calculator was the British ANITA Mk.VII, which used a Nixie tube display and 177 subminiature thyratron tubes. In June 1963, Friden introduced the four-function EC-130. It had an all-transistor design, 13-digit capacity on a 5-inch (130 mm) CRT, and introduced Reverse Polish notation (RPN) to the calculator market at a price of $2200. The EC-132 model added square root and reciprocal functions. In 1965, Wang Laboratories produced the LOCI-2, a 10-digit transistorized desktop calculator that used a Nixie tube display and could compute logarithms.

In the early days of binary vacuum-tube computers, their reliability was poor enough to justify marketing a mechanical octal version ("Binary Octal") of the Marchant desktop calculator. It was intended to check and verify calculation results of such computers.

Advanced Analog Computers

Before World War II, mechanical and electrical analog computers were considered the "state of the art", and many thought they were the future of computing. Analog computers take advantage of the strong similarities between the mathematics of small-scale properties—the position and motion of wheels or the voltage and current of electronic components—and the mathematics of other physical phenomena, for example, ballistic trajectories, inertia, resonance, energy transfer, momentum, and so forth. They model physical phenomena with electrical voltages and currents as the analog quantities.

Centrally, these analog systems work by creating electrical *analogs* of other systems, allowing users to predict behavior of the systems of interest by observing the electrical analogs. The most useful of the analogies was the way the small-scale behavior could be represented with integral and differential equations, and could be thus used to solve those equations. An ingenious example of such a machine, using water as the analog quantity, was the water integrator built in 1928; an electrical example is the Mallock machine built in 1941. A planimeter is a device which does integrals, using distance as the analog quantity. Unlike modern digital computers, analog computers are not very flexible, and need to be rewired manually to switch them from working on one problem to another. Analog computers had an advantage over early digital computers in that they could be used to solve complex problems using behavioral analogues while the earliest attempts at digital computers were quite limited.

Some of the most widely deployed analog computers included devices for aiming weapons, such as the Norden bombsight and the fire-control systems, such as Arthur Pollen's Argo system for naval vessels. Some stayed in use for decades after World War II; the Mark I Fire Control Computer was deployed by the United States Navy on a variety of ships from destroyers to battleships. Other analog computers included the Heathkit EC-1, and the hydraulic MONIAC Computer which modeled econometric flows.

The art of mechanical analog computing reached its zenith with the differential analyzer, built by H. L. Hazen and Vannevar Bush at MIT starting in 1927, which in turn built on the mechanical integrators invented in 1876 by James Thomson and the torque amplifiers invented by H. W. Nieman. A dozen of these devices were built before their obsolescence was obvious; the most powerful was constructed at the University of Pennsylvania's Moore School of Electrical Engineering, where the ENIAC was built. Digital electronic computers like the ENIAC spelled the end for most analog computing machines, but hybrid analog computers, controlled by digital electronics, remained in substantial use into the 1950s and 1960s, and later in some specialized applications. But like all digital devices, the decimal precision of a digital device is a limitation, as compared to an analog device, in which the accuracy is a limitation. As electronics progressed during the 20th century, its problems of operation at low voltages while maintaining high signal-to-noise ratios were steadily addressed, as shown below, for a digital circuit is a specialized form of analog circuit, intended to operate at standardized settings (continuing in the same vein, logic gates can be realized as forms of digital circuits). But as digital computers have become faster and use larger memory (for example, RAM or internal storage), they have almost entirely displaced analog computers. Computer programming, or coding, has arisen as another human profession.

Electronic Digital Computation

The era of modern computing began with a flurry of development before and during World War II, as electronic circuit elements replaced mechanical equivalents, and digital calculations replaced analog calculations. Machines such as the Z3, the Atanasoff–Berry Computer, the Colossus computers, and the ENIAC were built by hand using circuits containing relays or valves (vacuum tubes), and often used punched cards or punched paper tape for input and as the main (non-volatile) storage medium. Defining a single point in the series as the "first computer" misses many subtleties.

Alan Turing's 1936 paper proved enormously influential in computing and computer science in two ways. Its main purpose was to prove that there were problems (namely the halting problem) that could not be solved by any sequential process. In doing so, Turing provided a definition of a universal computer which executes a program stored on tape. This construct came to be called a Turing machine. Except for the limitations imposed by their finite memory stores, modern computers are said to be Turing-complete, which is to say, they have algorithm execution capability equivalent to a universal Turing machine.

For a computing machine to be a practical general-purpose computer, there must be some convenient read-write mechanism, punched tape, for example. With knowledge of Alan Turing's theoretical 'universal computing machine' John von Neumann defined an architecture which uses the same memory both to store programs and data: virtually all contemporary computers use this architecture (or some variant). While it is theoretically possible to implement a full computer entirely mechanically (as Babbage's design showed), electronics made possible the speed and later the miniaturization that characterize modern computers.

There were three parallel streams of computer development in the World War II era; the first stream largely ignored, and the second stream deliberately kept secret. The first was the German work of Konrad Zuse. The second was the secret development of the Colossus computers in the UK. Neither of these had much influence on the various computing projects in the United States. The third stream of computer development, Eckert and Mauchly's ENIAC and EDVAC, was widely publicized.

George Stibitz is internationally recognized as one of the fathers of the modern digital computer. While working at Bell Labs in November 1937, Stibitz invented and built a relay-based calculator that he dubbed the "Model K" (for "kitchen table", on which he had assembled it), which was the first to calculate using binary form.

Zuse

Working in isolation in Germany, Konrad Zuse started construction in 1936 of his first Z-series calculators featuring memory and (initially limited) programmability. Zuse's purely mechanical, but already binary Z1, finished in 1938, never worked reliably due to problems with the precision of parts.

Zuse's later machine, the Z3, was finished in 1941. It was based on telephone relays and did work satisfactorily. The Z3 thus became the first functional program-controlled, all-purpose, digital computer. In many ways it was quite similar to modern machines, pioneering numerous advances, such as floating point numbers. Replacement of the hard-to-implement decimal system (used in Charles Babbage's earlier design) by the simpler binary system meant that Zuse's machines were easier to build and potentially more reliable, given the technologies available at that time.

Programs were fed into Z3 on punched films. Conditional jumps were missing, but since the 1990s it has been proved theoretically that Z3 was still a universal computer (as always, ignoring physical storage limitations).

In two 1936 patent applications, Konrad Zuse also anticipated that machine instructions could be stored in the same storage used for data—the key insight of what became known as the von Neumann architecture, first implemented in the British SSEM of 1948. Zuse also claimed to have designed the first higher-level programming language, which he named Plankalkül, in 1945 (published in 1948) although it was implemented for the first time in 2000 by a team around Raúl Rojas at the Free University of Berlin—five years after Zuse died.

Zuse suffered setbacks during World War II when some of his machines were destroyed in the course of Allied bombing campaigns. Apparently his work remained largely unknown to engineers in the UK and US until much later, although at least IBM was aware of it as it financed his post-war startup company in 1946 in return for an option on Zuse's patents.

Colossus

During World War II, the British at Bletchley Park (40 miles north of London) achieved a number of successes at breaking encrypted German military communications. The German encryption machine, Enigma, was attacked with the help of electro-mechanical machines called *bombes*. The bombe, designed by Alan Turing and Gordon Welchman, after the Polish cryptographic *bomba* by Marian Rejewski (1938), came into productive use in 1941. They ruled out possible Enigma settings by performing chains of logical deductions implemented electrically. Most possibilities led to a contradiction, and the few remaining could be tested by hand.

The Germans also developed a series of teleprinter encryption systems, quite different from Enigma. The Lorenz SZ 40/42 machine was used for high-level Army communications, termed "Tunny" by the British. The first intercepts of Lorenz messages began in 1941. As part of an attack on Tunny, Professor Max Newman and his colleagues helped specify the Colossus. The Mk I Colossus was built between March and December 1943 by Tommy Flowers and his colleagues at the Post Office Research Station at Dollis Hill in London and then shipped to Bletchley Park in January 1944.

Colossus was the world's first electronic programmable computing device. It used a large number of valves (vacuum tubes). It had paper-tape input and was capable of being configured to perform a variety of boolean logical operations on its data, but it was not Turing-complete. Nine Mk II Colossi were built (The Mk I was converted to a Mk II making ten machines in total). Details of their existence, design, and use were kept secret well into the 1970s. Winston Churchill personally issued an order for their destruction into pieces no larger than a man's hand, to keep secret that the British were capable of cracking Lorenz during the oncoming cold war. As a result the machines were not included in many histories of computing. A reconstructed copy of one of the Colossus machines is now on display at Bletchley Park.

American Developments

In 1937, Claude Shannon showed there is a one-to-one correspondence between the concepts of Boolean logic and certain electrical circuits, now called logic gates, which are now ubiquitous in digital computers. In his master's thesis at MIT, for the first time in history, Shannon showed that electronic relays and switches can realize the expressions of Boolean algebra. Entitled *A Symbolic Analysis of Relay and Switching Circuits*, Shannon's thesis essentially founded practical digital circuit design. George Stibitz completed a relay-based computer he dubbed the "Model K" at Bell Labs in November 1937. Bell Labs authorized a full research program in late 1938 with Stibitz at the helm. Their *Complex Number Calculator*, completed January 8, 1940, was able to calculate complex numbers. In a demonstration to the American Mathematical Society conference at Dartmouth College on September 11, 1940, Stibitz was able to send the Complex Number Calculator remote commands over telephone lines by a teletype. It was the first computing machine ever used remotely, in this case over a phone line. Some participants in the conference who witnessed the demonstration were John von Neumann, John Mauchly, and Norbert Wiener, who wrote about it in their memoirs.

In 1939, John Vincent Atanasoff and Clifford E. Berry of Iowa State University developed the Atanasoff–Berry Computer (ABC), The Atanasoff-Berry Computer was the world's first electronic digital computer. The design used over 300 vacuum tubes and employed capacitors fixed in a mechanically rotating drum for memory. Though the ABC machine was not programmable, it was the first to use electronic tubes in an adder. ENIAC co-inventor John Mauchly examined the ABC in June 1941, and its influence on the design of the later ENIAC machine is a matter of contention among computer historians. The ABC was largely forgotten until it became the focus of the lawsuit *Honeywell v. Sperry Rand*, the ruling of which invalidated the ENIAC patent (and several others) as, among many reasons, having been anticipated by Atanasoff's work.

In 1939, development began at IBM's Endicott laboratories on the Harvard Mark I. Known officially as the Automatic Sequence Controlled Calculator, the Mark I was a general purpose electro-mechanical computer built with IBM financing and with assistance from IBM personnel, under the direction of Harvard mathematician Howard Aiken. Its design was influenced by Babbage's Analytical Engine, using decimal arithmetic and storage wheels and rotary switches in addition to electromagnetic relays. It was programmable via punched paper tape, and contained several calculation units working in parallel. Later versions contained several paper tape readers and the machine could switch between readers based on a condition. Nevertheless, the machine was not quite Turing-complete. The Mark I was moved to Harvard University and began operation in May 1944.

Eniac

The US-built ENIAC (Electronic Numerical Integrator and Computer) was the first electronic general-purpose computer. It combined, for the first time, the high speed of electronics with the ability to be programmed for many complex problems. It could add or subtract 5000 times a second, a thousand times faster than any other machine. (Colossus couldn't add). It also had modules to multiply, divide, and square root. High speed memory was limited to 20 words (about 80 bytes). Built under the direction of John Mauchly and J. Presper Eckert at the University of Pennsylvania, ENIAC's development and construction lasted from 1943 to full operation at the end of 1945. The machine was huge, weighing 30 tons, and contained over 18,000 vacuum tubes. One of the major engineering feats was to minimize tube burnout, which was a common problem at that time. The machine was in almost constant use for the next ten years.

ENIAC was unambiguously a Turing-complete device. It could compute any problem (that would fit in memory). A "program" on the ENIAC, however, was defined by the states of its patch cables and switches, a far cry from the stored program electronic machines that evolved from it. Once a program was written, it had to be mechanically set into the machine. Six women did most of the programming of ENIAC. (Improvements completed in 1948 made it possible to execute stored programs set in function table memory, which made programming less a "one-off" effort, and more systematic).

First-generation Machines

Even before the ENIAC was finished, Eckert and Mauchly recognized its limitations and started the design of a stored-program computer, EDVAC. John von Neumann was credited with a widely circulated report describing the EDVAC design in which both the programs and working data were stored in a single, unified store. This basic design, denoted the von Neumann architecture, would serve as the foundation for the worldwide development of ENIAC's successors. In this generation of equipment, temporary or working storage was provided by acoustic delay lines, which used the propagation time of sound through a medium such as liquid mercury (or through a wire) to briefly store data. A series of acoustic pulses is sent along a tube; after a time, as the pulse reached the end of the tube, the circuitry detected whether the pulse represented a 1 or 0 and caused the oscillator to re-send the pulse. Others used Williams tubes, which use the ability of a small cathode-ray tube (CRT) to store and retrieve data as charged areas on the phosphor screen. By 1954, magnetic core memory was rapidly displacing most other forms of temporary storage, and dominated the field through the mid-1970s.

EDVAC was the first stored-program computer designed; however it was not the first to run. Eckert and Mauchly left the project and its construction floundered. The first working von Neumann machine was the Manchester "Baby" or Small-Scale Experimental Machine, developed by Frederic C. Williams and Tom Kilburn at the University of Manchester in 1948 as a test bed for the Williams tube; it was followed in 1949 by the Manchester Mark 1 computer, a complete system, using Williams tube and magnetic drum memory, and introducing index registers. The other contender for the title "first digital stored-program computer" had been EDSAC, designed and constructed at the University of Cambridge. Operational less than one year after the Manchester "Baby", it was also capable of tackling real problems. EDSAC was actually inspired by plans for EDVAC (Electronic Discrete Variable Automatic Computer), the successor to ENIAC; these plans were already in place by the time ENIAC was successfully operational. Unlike ENIAC, which used parallel processing, EDVAC used a single processing unit. This design was simpler and was the first to be implemented in each succeeding wave of miniaturization, and increased reliability. Some view Manchester Mark 1 / EDSAC / EDVAC as the "Eves" from which nearly all current computers derive their architecture. Manchester University's machine became the prototype for the Ferranti Mark 1. The first Ferranti Mark 1 machine was delivered to the University in February, 1951 and at least nine others were sold between 1951 and 1957.

The first universal programmable computer in the Soviet Union was created by a team of scientists under direction of Sergei Alekseyevich Lebedev from Kiev Institute of Electrotechnology, Soviet Union (now Ukraine). The computer MESM (*ÌÝÑÌ, Small Electronic Calculating Machine*) became operational in 1950. It had about 6,000 vacuum tubes and consumed 25 kW of power. It could perform approximately 3,000 operations per second. Another early machine was CSIRAC, an Australian design that ran its first test program in 1949. CSIRAC is the oldest computer still in existence and the first to have been used to play digital music.

Commercial Computers

The first commercial computer was the Ferranti Mark 1, which was delivered to the University of Manchester in

February 1951. It was based on the Manchester Mark 1. The main improvements over the Manchester Mark 1 were in the size of the primary storage (using random access Williams tubes), secondary storage (using a magnetic drum), a faster multiplier, and additional instructions. The basic cycle time was 1.2 milliseconds, and a multiplication could be completed in about 2.16 milliseconds. The multiplier used almost a quarter of the machine's 4,050 vacuum tubes (valves). A second machine was purchased by the University of Toronto, before the design was revised into the Mark 1 Star. At least seven of these later machines were delivered between 1953 and 1957, one of them to Shell labs in Amsterdam.

In October 1947, the directors of J. Lyons & Company, a British catering company famous for its teashops but with strong interests in new office management techniques, decided to take an active role in promoting the commercial development of computers. The LEO I computer became operational in April 1951 and ran the world's first regular routine office computer job. On 17 November 1951, the J. Lyons company began weekly operation of a bakery valuations job on the LEO (Lyons Electronic Office). This was the first business application to go live on a stored program computer.

In June 1951, the UNIVAC I (Universal Automatic Computer) was delivered to the U.S. Census Bureau. Remington Rand eventually sold 46 machines at more than $1 million each ($8.46 million as of 2011). UNIVAC was the first "mass produced" computer. It used 5,200 vacuum tubes and consumed 125 kW of power. Its primary storage was serial-access mercury delay lines capable of storing 1,000 words of 11 decimal digits plus sign (72-bit words). A key feature of the UNIVAC system was a newly invented type of metal magnetic tape, and a high-speed tape unit, for non-volatile storage. Magnetic media are still used in many computers. In 1952, IBM publicly announced the IBM 701 Electronic Data Processing Machine, the first in its successful 700/7000 series and its first IBM mainframe computer. The IBM 704, introduced in 1954, used magnetic core memory, which became the standard for large machines. The first implemented high-level general purpose programming language, Fortran, was also being developed at IBM for the 704 during 1955 and 1956 and released in early 1957. (Konrad Zuse's 1945 design of the high-level language Plankalkül was not implemented at that time.) A volunteer user group, which exists to this day, was founded in 1955 to share their software and experiences with the IBM 701.

IBM introduced a smaller, more affordable computer in 1954 that proved very popular. The IBM 650 weighed over 900 kg, the attached power supply weighed around 1350 kg and both were held in separate cabinets of roughly 1.5 meters by 0.9 meters by 1.8 meters. It cost $500,000 ($4.09 million as of 2011) or could be leased for $3,500 a month ($30 thousand as of 2011). Its drum memory was originally 2,000 ten-digit words, later expanded to 4,000 words. Memory limitations such as this were to dominate programming for decades afterward. The program instructions were fetched from the spinning drum as the code ran. Efficient execution using drum memory was provided by a combination of hardware architecture: the instruction format included the address of the next instruction; and software: the Symbolic Optimal Assembly Program, SOAP, assigned instructions to the optimal addresses (to the extent possible by static analysis of the source program). Thus many instructions were, when needed, located in the next row of the drum to be read and additional wait time for drum rotation was not required.

In 1955, Maurice Wilkes invented microprogramming, which allows the base instruction set to be defined or extended by built-in programs (now called firmware or microcode). It was widely used in the CPUs and floating-point units of mainframe and other computers, such as the Manchester Atlas and the IBM 360 series.

IBM introduced its first magnetic disk system, RAMAC (Random Access Method of Accounting and Control) in 1956. Using fifty 24-inch (610 mm) metal disks, with 100 tracks per side, it was able to store 5 megabytes of data at a cost of $10,000 per megabyte ($80 thousand as of 2011).

Second Feneration: Transistors

The bipolar transistor was invented in 1947. From 1955 onwards transistors replaced vacuum tubes in computer designs, giving rise to the "second generation" of computers. Initially the only devices available were germanium point-contact transistors, which although less reliable than the vacuum tubes they replaced had the advantage of consuming far less power. The first transistorised computer was built at the University of Manchester and was operational by 1953; a second version was completed there in April 1955. The later machine used 200 transistors and 1,300 solid-state diodes and had a power consumption of 150 watts. However, it still required valves to generate the clock waveforms at 125 kHz and to read and write on the magnetic drum memory, whereas the Harwell CADET operated without any valves by using a lower clock frequency, of 58 kHz when it became operational in February 1955. Problems with the reliability of early batches of point contact and alloyed junction transistors meant that the machine's mean time between failures was about 90 minutes, but this improved once the more reliable bipolar junction transistors became available.

Compared to vacuum tubes, transistors have many advantages: they are smaller, and require less power than vacuum tubes, so give off less heat. Silicon junction transistors were much more reliable than vacuum tubes and had longer, indefinite, service life. Transistorized computers could contain tens of thousands of binary logic circuits in a relatively compact space. Transistors greatly reduced computers' size, initial cost, and operating cost. Typically, second-generation computers were composed of large numbers of printed circuit boards such as the IBM Standard Modular System each carrying one to four logic gates or flip-flops.

A second generation computer, the IBM 1401, captured about one third of the world market. IBM installed more than ten thousand 1401s between 1960 and 1964.

Transistorized electronics improved not only the CPU (Central Processing Unit), but also the peripheral devices. The IBM 350 RAMAC was introduced in 1956 and was the world's first disk drive. The second generation disk data storage units were able to store tens of millions of letters and digits. Next to the fixed disk storage units, connected to the CPU via high-speed data transmission, were removable disk data storage units. A removable disk stack can be easily exchanged with another stack in a few seconds. Even if the removable disks' capacity is smaller than fixed disks, their interchangeability guarantees a nearly unlimited quantity of data close at hand. Magnetic tape provided archival capability for this data, at a lower cost than disk.

Many second-generation CPUs delegated peripheral device communications to a secondary processor. For example, while the communication processor controlled card reading and punching, the main CPU executed calculations and binary branch instructions. One databus would bear data between the main CPU and core memory at the CPU's fetch-execute cycle rate, and other databusses would typically serve the peripheral devices. On the PDP-1, the core memory's cycle time was 5 microseconds;

consequently most arithmetic instructions took 10 microseconds (100,000 operations per second) because most operations took at least two memory cycles; one for the instruction, one for the operand data fetch.

During the second generation remote terminal units (often in the form of teletype machines like a Friden Flexowriter) saw greatly increased use. Telephone connections provided sufficient speed for early remote terminals and allowed hundreds of kilometers separation between remote-terminals and the computing center. Eventually these stand-alone computer networks would be generalized into an interconnected *network of networks*—the Internet.

Post-1960: Third Generation and Beyond

The explosion in the use of computers began with "third-generation" computers, making use of Jack St. Clair Kilby's and Robert Noyce's independent invention of the integrated circuit (or microchip), which led to the invention of the microprocessor, by Ted Hoff, Federico Faggin, and Stanley Mazor at Intel. The integrated circuit in the image on the right, for example, an Intel 8742, is an 8-bit microcontroller that includes a CPU running at 12 MHz, 128 bytes of RAM, 2048 bytes of EPROM, and I/O in the same chip.

During the 1960s there was considerable overlap between second and third generation technologies. IBM implemented its IBM Solid Logic Technology modules in hybrid circuits for the IBM System/360 in 1964. As late as 1975, Sperry Univac continued the manufacture of second-generation machines such as the UNIVAC 494. The Burroughs large systems such as the B5000 were stack machines, which allowed for simpler programming. These pushdown automatons were also implemented in minicomputers and microprocessors later, which influenced programming language design. Minicomputers served as low-cost computer centers for industry, business and universities. It became possible to simulate analog circuits with the *simulation program with integrated circuit emphasis*, or SPICE (1971) on minicomputers, one of the programs for electronic design automation (EDA). The microprocessor led to the development of the microcomputer, small, low-cost computers that could be owned by individuals and small businesses. Microcomputers, the first of which appeared in the 1970s, became ubiquitous in the 1980s and beyond.

In April 1975 at the Hannover Fair, was presented the P6060 produced by Olivetti, the world's first personal with built-in floppy disk: Central Unit on two plates, code names PUCE1/PUCE2, TTL components made, 8" single or double floppy disk driver, 32 alphanumeric characters plasma display, 80 columns graphical thermal printer, 48 Kbytes of RAM, Basic language, 40 kilograms of weight. He was in competition with a similar product by IBM but with an external floppy disk.

Steve Wozniak, co-founder of Apple Computer, is sometimes erroneously credited with developing the first mass-market home computers. However, his first computer, the Apple I, came out some time after the MOS Technology KIM-1 and Altair 8800, and the first Apple computer with graphic and sound capabilities came out well after the Commodore PET. Computing has evolved with microcomputer architectures, with features added from their larger brethren, now dominant in most market segments.

Systems as complicated as computers require very high reliability. ENIAC remained on, in continuous operation from 1947 to 1955, for eight years before being shut down. Although a vacuum tube might fail, it would be replaced without bringing down the system. By the simple strategy of never shutting down ENIAC, the failures were dramatically reduced. The vacuum-tube SAGE air-defense computers became remarkably reliable – installed in pairs, one off-line, tubes likely to fail did so when the computer was intentionally run at reduced power to find them. Hot-pluggable hard disks, like the hot-pluggable vacuum tubes of yesteryear, continue the tradition of repair during continuous operation. Semiconductor memories routinely have no errors when they operate, although operating systems like Unix have employed memory tests on start-up to detect failing hardware. Today, the requirement of reliable performance is made even more stringent when server farms are the delivery platform. Google has managed this by using fault-tolerant software to recover from hardware failures, and is even working on the concept of replacing entire server farms on-the-fly, during a service event.

In the 21st century, multi-core CPUs became commercially available. Content-addressable memory (CAM) has become inexpensive enough to be used in networking, although no computer system has yet implemented hardware CAMs for use in programming languages. Currently, CAMs (or associative arrays) in software are programming-language-specific. Semiconductor memory cell arrays are very regular structures, and manufacturers prove their processes on them; this allows price reductions on memory products. During the 1980s, CMOS logic gates developed into devices that could be made as fast as other circuit types; computer power consumption could therefore be decreased dramatically. Unlike the continuous current draw of a gate based on other logic types, a CMOS gate only draws significant current during the 'transition' between logic states, except for leakage.

This has allowed computing to become a commodity which is now ubiquitous, embedded in many forms, from greeting cards and telephones to satellites. Computing hardware and its software have even become a metaphor for the operation of the universe. Although DNA-based computing and quantum qubit computing are years or decades in the future, the infrastructure is being laid today, for example, with DNA origami on photolithography and with quantum antennae for transferring information between ion traps. Fast digital circuits (including those based on Josephson junctions and rapid single flux quantum technology) are becoming more nearly realizable with the discovery of nanoscale superconductors.

Fiber-optic and photonic devices, which already have been used to transport data over long distances, are now entering the data center, side by side with CPU and semiconductor memory components. This allows the separation of RAM from CPU by optical interconnects.

An indication of the rapidity of development of this field can be inferred by the history of the seminal article. By the time that anyone had time to write anything down, it was obsolete. After 1945, others read John von Neumann's *First Draft of a Report on the EDVAC*, and immediately started implementing their own systems. To this day, the pace of development has continued, worldwide.

Programs

The defining feature of modern computers which distinguishes them from all other machines is that they can be programmed. That is to say that some type of instructions (the program) can be given to the computer, and it will carry process them. While some computers may have strange concepts "instructions" and "output", modern computers based on the von Neumann architecture are often have machine code in the form of an imperative programming language.

In practical terms, a computer program may be just a few instructions or extend to many millions of instructions, as do the programs for word processors and web browsers for example. A typical modern computer can execute billions of instructions per second (gigaflops) and rarely makes a mistake over many years of operation. Large computer programs consisting of several million instructions may take teams of programmers years to write, and due to the complexity of the task almost certainly contain errors.

Stored Program Architecture

This section applies to most common RAM machine-based computers. In most cases, computer instructions are simple: add one number to another, move some data from one location to another, send a message to some external device, etc. These instructions are read from the computer's memory and are generally carried out (executed) in the order they were given. However, there are usually specialized instructions to tell the computer to jump ahead or backwards to some other place in the program and to carry on executing from there. These are called "jump" instructions (or branches). Furthermore, jump instructions may be made to happen conditionally so that different sequences of instructions may be used depending on the result of some previous calculation or some external event. Many computers directly support subroutines by providing a type of jump that "remembers" the location it jumped from and another instruction to return to the instruction following that jump instruction.

Program execution might be likened to reading a book. While a person will normally read each word and line in sequence, they may at times jump back to an earlier place in the text or skip sections that are not of interest. Similarly, a computer may sometimes go back and repeat the instructions in some section of the program over and over again until some internal condition is met. This is called the flow of control within the program and it is what allows the computer to perform tasks repeatedly without human intervention.

Comparatively, a person using a pocket calculator can perform a basic arithmetic operation such as adding two numbers with just a few button presses. But to add together all of the numbers from 1 to 1,000 would take thousands of button presses and a lot of time—with a near certainty of making a mistake. On the other hand, a computer may be programmed to do this with just a few simple instructions.

Bugs

Errors in computer programs are called "bugs". Bugs may be benign and not affect the usefulness of the program, or have only subtle effects. But in some cases they may cause the program to "hang"—become unresponsive to input such as mouse clicks or keystrokes, or to completely fail or "crash". Otherwise benign bugs may sometimes be harnessed for malicious intent by an unscrupulous user writing an "exploit"—code designed to take advantage of a bug and disrupt a computer's proper execution. Bugs are usually not the fault of the computer. Since computers merely execute the instructions they are given, bugs are nearly always the result of programmer error or an oversight made in the program's design. Rear Admiral Grace Hopper is credited for having first used the term 'bugs' in computing after a dead moth was found shorting a relay of the Harvard Mark II computer in September 1947.

Machine Code

In most computers, individual instructions are stored as machine code with each instruction being given a unique number (its operation code or opcode for short). The command to add two numbers together would have one opcode, the command to multiply them would have a different opcode and so on. The simplest computers are able to perform any of a handful of different instructions; the more complex computers have several hundred to choose from—each with a unique numerical code. Since the computer's memory is able to store numbers, it can also store the instruction codes. This leads to the important fact that entire programs (which are just lists of these instructions) can be represented as lists of numbers and can themselves be manipulated inside the computer in the same way as numeric data. The fundamental concept of storing programs in the computer's memory alongside the data they operate on is the crux of the von Neumann, or stored program, architecture. In some cases, a computer might store some or all of its program in memory that is kept separate from the data it operates on. This is called the Harvard architecture after the Harvard Mark I computer. Modern von Neumann computers display some traits of the Harvard architecture in their designs, such as in CPU caches.

While it is possible to write computer programs as long lists of numbers (machine language) and while this technique was used with many early computers, it is extremely tedious and potentially error-prone to do so in practice, especially for complicated programs. Instead, each basic instruction can be given a short name that is indicative of its function and easy to remember—a mnemonic such as ADD, SUB, MULT or JUMP. These mnemonics are collectively known as a computer's assembly language. Converting programs written in assembly language into something the computer can actually understand (machine language) is usually done by a computer program called an assembler. Machine languages and the assembly languages that represent them (collectively termed low-level programming languages) tend to be unique to a particular type of computer. For instance, an ARM architecture computer (such as may be found in a PDA or a hand-held videogame) cannot understand the machine language of an Intel Pentium or the AMD Athlon 64 computer that might be in a PC.

Higher-level Languages and Program Design

Though considerably easier than in machine language, writing long programs in assembly language is often difficult and is also error prone. Therefore, most practical programs are written in more abstract high-level programming languages that are able to express the needs of the programmer more conveniently (and thereby help reduce programmer error). High level languages are usually "compiled" into machine language (or sometimes into assembly language and then into machine language) using another computer program called a compiler. High level languages are less related to the workings of the target computer than assembly language, and more related to the language and structure of the problem(s) to be solved by the final program. It is therefore often possible to use different compilers to translate the same high level language program into the machine language of many different types of computer. This is part of the means by which software like video games may be made available for different computer architectures such as personal computers and various video game consoles.

The task of developing large software systems presents a significant intellectual challenge. Producing software with an acceptably high reliability within a predictable schedule and budget has historically been difficult; the academic and professional discipline of software engineering concentrates specifically on this challenge.

Function

A general purpose computer has four main components: the arithmetic logic unit (ALU), the control unit, the memory, and the input and output devices (collectively termed I/O). These parts are interconnected by busses, often made of groups of wires.

Inside each of these parts are thousands to trillions of small electrical circuits which can be turned off or on by means of an electronic switch. Each circuit represents a bit (binary digit) of information so that when the circuit is on it represents a "1", and when off it represents a "0" (in positive logic representation). The circuits are arranged in logic gates so that one or more of the circuits may control the state of one or more of the other circuits.

The control unit, ALU, registers, and basic I/O (and often other hardware closely linked with these) are collectively known as a central processing unit (CPU). Early CPUs were composed of many separate components but since the mid-1970s CPUs have typically been constructed on a single integrated circuit called a *microprocessor*.

Control Unit

The control unit (often called a control system or central controller) manages the computer's various components; it reads and interprets (decodes) the program instructions, transforming them into a series of control signals which activate other parts of the computer. Control systems in advanced computers may change the order of some instructions so as to improve performance.

A key component common to all CPUs is the program counter, a special memory cell (a register) that keeps track of which location in memory the next instruction is to be read from.

The control system's function is as follows—note that this is a simplified description, and some of these steps may be performed concurrently or in a different order depending on the type of CPU:

1. Read the code for the next instruction from the cell indicated by the program counter.
2. Decode the numerical code for the instruction into a set of commands or signals for each of the other systems.
3. Increment the program counter so it points to the next instruction.
4. Read whatever data the instruction requires from cells in memory (or perhaps from an input device). The location of this required data is typically stored within the instruction code.
5. Provide the necessary data to an ALU or register.
6. If the instruction requires an ALU or specialized hardware to complete, instruct the hardware to perform the requested operation.
7. Write the result from the ALU back to a memory location or to a register or perhaps an output device.
8. Jump back to step (1).

Since the program counter is (conceptually) just another set of memory cells, it can be changed by calculations done in the ALU. Adding 100 to the program counter would cause the next instruction to be read from a place 100 locations further down the program. Instructions that modify the program counter are often known as "jumps" and allow for loops (instructions that are repeated by the computer) and often conditional instruction execution (both examples of control flow).

It is noticeable that the sequence of operations that the control unit goes through to process an instruction is in itself like a short computer program—and indeed, in some more complex CPU designs, there is another yet smaller computer called a microsequencer that runs a microcode program that causes all of these events to happen.

Arithmetic/logic Unit (ALU)

The ALU is capable of performing two classes of operations: arithmetic and logic.

The set of arithmetic operations that a particular ALU supports may be limited to adding and subtracting or might include multiplying or dividing, trigonometry functions (sine, cosine, etc.) and square roots. Some can only operate on whole numbers (integers) whilst others use floating point to represent real numbers—albeit with limited precision. However, any computer that is capable of performing just the simplest operations can be programmed to break down the more complex operations into simple steps that it can perform. Therefore, any computer can be programmed to perform any arithmetic operation—although it will take more time to do so if its ALU does not directly support the operation. An ALU may also compare numbers and return boolean truth values (true or false) depending on whether one is equal to, greater than or less than the other.

Logic operations involve Boolean logic: AND, OR, XOR and NOT. These can be useful both for creating complicated conditional statements and processing boolean logic. Superscalar computers may contain multiple ALUs so that they can process several instructions at the same time. Graphics processors and computers with SIMD and MIMD features often provide ALUs that can perform arithmetic on vectors and matrices.

Memory

A computer's memory can be viewed as a list of cells into which numbers can be placed or read. Each cell has a numbered "address" and can store a single number. The computer can be instructed to "put the number 123 into the cell numbered 1357" or to "add the number that is in cell 1357 to the number that is in cell 2468 and put the answer into cell 1595". The information stored in memory may represent practically anything. Letters, numbers, even computer instructions can be placed into memory with equal ease. Since the CPU does not differentiate between different types of information, it is the software's responsibility to give significance to what the memory sees as nothing but a series of numbers.

In almost all modern computers, each memory cell is set up to store binary numbers in groups of eight bits (called a byte). Each byte is able to represent 256 different numbers (2^8 = 256); either from 0 to 255 or "128 to +127. To store larger numbers, several consecutive bytes may be used (typically, two, four or eight). When negative numbers are required, they are usually stored in two's complement notation. Other arrangements are possible, but are usually not seen outside of specialized applications or historical contexts. A computer can store any kind of information in memory if it can be represented numerically. Modern computers have billions or even trillions of bytes of memory.

The CPU contains a special set of memory cells called registers that can be read and written to much more rapidly than the main memory area. There are typically between two and one hundred registers depending on the type of CPU. Registers are used for the most frequently needed data items to avoid having to access main memory every time data is needed. As data is constantly being worked on, reducing the need to access main memory (which is often slow compared to the ALU and control units) greatly increases the computer's speed.

Computer main memory comes in two principal varieties: random-access memory or RAM and read-only memory or ROM. RAM can be read and written to anytime the CPU commands it, but ROM is pre-loaded with data and software that never changes, so the CPU can only read from it. ROM is typically used to store the computer's initial start-up instructions. In general, the contents of RAM are erased when the power to the computer is turned off, but ROM retains its data indefinitely. In a PC, the ROM contains a specialized program called the BIOS that orchestrates loading the computer's operating system from the hard disk drive into RAM whenever the computer is turned on or reset. In embedded computers, which frequently do not have disk drives, all of the required software may be stored in ROM. Software stored in ROM is often called firmware, because it is notionally more like hardware than software. Flash memory blurs the distinction between ROM and RAM, as it retains its data when turned off but is also rewritable. It is typically much slower than conventional ROM and RAM however, so its use is restricted to applications where high speed is unnecessary.

In more sophisticated computers there may be one or more RAM cache memories which are slower than registers but faster than main memory. Generally computers with this sort of cache are designed to move frequently needed data into the cache automatically, often without the need for any intervention on the programmer's part.

Input/output (I/O)

I/O is the means by which a computer exchanges information with the outside world. Devices that provide input or output to the computer are called peripherals. On a typical personal computer, peripherals include input devices like the keyboard and mouse, and output devices such as the display and printer. Hard disk drives, floppy disk drives and optical disc drives serve as both input and output devices. Computer networking is another form of I/O.

Often, I/O devices are complex computers in their own right with their own CPU and memory. A graphics processing unit might contain fifty or more tiny computers that perform the calculations necessary to display 3D graphics. Modern desktop computers contain many smaller computers that assist the main CPU in performing I/O.

Multitasking

While a computer may be viewed as running one gigantic program stored in its main memory, in some systems it is necessary to give the appearance of running several programs simultaneously. This is achieved by multitasking i.e. having the computer switch rapidly between running each program in turn.

One means by which this is done is with a special signal called an interrupt which can periodically cause the computer to stop executing instructions where it was and do something else instead. By remembering where it was executing prior to the interrupt, the computer can return to that task later. If several programs are running "at the same time", then the interrupt generator might be causing several hundred interrupts per second, causing a program switch each time. Since modern computers typically execute instructions several orders of magnitude faster than human perception, it may appear that many programs are running at the same time even though only one is ever executing in any given instant. This method of multitasking is sometimes termed "time-sharing" since each program is allocated a "slice" of time in turn.

Before the era of cheap computers, the principal use for multitasking was to allow many people to share the same computer. Seemingly, multitasking would cause a computer that is switching between several programs to run more slowly — in direct proportion to the number of programs it is running. However, most programs spend much of their time waiting for slow input/output devices to complete their tasks. If a program is waiting for the user to click on the mouse or press a key on the keyboard, then it will not take a "time slice" until the event it is waiting for has occurred. This frees up time for other programs to execute so that many programs may be run at the same time without unacceptable speed loss.

Multiprocessing

Some computers are designed to distribute their work across several CPUs in a multiprocessing configuration, a technique once employed only in large and powerful machines such as supercomputers, mainframe computers and servers. Multiprocessor and multi-core (multiple CPUs on a single integrated circuit) personal and laptop computers are now widely available, and are being increasingly used in lower-end markets as a result.

Supercomputers in particular often have highly unique architectures that differ significantly from the basic stored-program architecture and from general purpose computers. They often feature thousands of CPUs, customized high-speed interconnects, and specialized computing hardware. Such designs tend to be useful only for specialized tasks due to the large scale of program organization required to successfully utilize most of the available resources at once. Supercomputers usually see usage in large-scale simulation, graphics rendering, and cryptography applications, as well as with other so-called "embarrassingly parallel" tasks.

Networking and the Internet

Computers have been used to coordinate information between multiple locations since the 1950s. The U.S. military's SAGE system was the first large-scale example of such a system, which led to a number of special-purpose commercial systems like Sabre.

In the 1970s, computer engineers at research institutions throughout the United States began to link their computers together using telecommunications technology. This effort was funded by ARPA (now DARPA), and the computer network that it produced was called the ARPANET. The technologies that made the Arpanet possible spread and evolved.

In time, the network spread beyond academic and military institutions and became known as the Internet. The emergence of networking involved a redefinition of the nature and boundaries of the computer. Computer operating systems and applications were modified to include the ability to define and access the resources of other computers on the network, such as peripheral devices, stored information, and the like, as extensions of the resources of an individual computer. Initially these facilities were available primarily to people working in high-tech environments, but in the 1990s the spread of applications like e-mail and the World Wide Web, combined with the development of cheap, fast networking technologies like Ethernet and ADSL saw computer networking become almost ubiquitous. In fact, the number of computers that are networked is growing phenomenally. A very large proportion of personal computers regularly connect to the Internet to communicate and receive information. "Wireless" networking, often utilizing mobile phone networks, has meant networking is becoming increasingly ubiquitous even in mobile computing environments.

Misconceptions

A computer does not need to be electric, nor even have a processor, nor RAM, nor even hard disk. The minimal definition of a computer is anything that transforms information in a purposeful way. However the traditional definition of a computer is a device having memory, mass storage, processor (CPU), and Input & Output devices. Anything less would be a simple processor.

Required Technology

Computational systems as flexible as a personal computer can be built out of almost anything. For example, a computer can be made out of billiard balls (billiard ball computer); this is an unintuitive and pedagogical example that a computer can be made out of almost anything. More realistically, modern computers are made out of transistors made of photolithographed semiconductors. Historically, computers evolved from mechanical computers and eventually from vacuum tubes to transistors.

There is active research to make computers out of many promising new types of technology, such as optical computing, DNA computers, neural computers, and quantum computers. Some of these can easily tackle problems that modern computers cannot (such as how quantum computers can break some modern encryption algorithms by quantum factoring).

Computer Architecture Paradigms

Some different paradigms of how to build a computer from the ground-up:

RAM Machines

These are the types of computers with a CPU, computer memory, etc., which understand basic instructions in a machine language. The concept evolved from the Turing machine.

Brains

Brains are massively parallel processors made of neurons, wired in intricate patterns, that communicate via electricity and neurotransmitter chemicals.

Programming Languages

Such as the lambda calculus, or modern programming languages, are virtual computers built on top of other computers.

Cellular Automata

For example, the game of Life can create "gliders" and "loops" and other constructs that transmit information; this paradigm can be applied to DNA computing, chemical computing, etc.

Groups and Committees

The linking of multiple computers (brains) is itself a computer. Logic gates are a common abstraction which can apply to most of the above digital or analog paradigms.

The ability to store and execute lists of instructions called programs makes computers extremely versatile, distinguishing them from calculators. The Church–Turing thesis is a mathematical statement of this versatility: any computer with a minimum capability (being Turing-complete) is, in principle, capable of performing the same tasks that any other computer can perform. Therefore any type of computer (netbook, supercomputer, cellular automaton, etc.) is able to perform the same computational tasks, given enough time and storage capacity.

Limited-function Computers

Conversely, a computer which is limited in function (one that is not "Turing-complete") cannot simulate arbitrary things. For example, simple four-function calculators cannot simulate a real computer without human intervention. As a more complicated example, without the ability to program a gaming console, it can never accomplish what a programmable calculator from the 1990s could (given enough time); the system as a whole is not Turing-complete, even though it contains a Turing-complete component (the microprocessor). Living organisms (the body, not the brain) are also limited-function computers designed to make copies of themselves; they cannot be reprogrammed without genetic engineering.

Virtual Computers

A "computer" is commonly considered to be a physical device. However, one can create a computer program which describes how to run a different computer, i.e. "simulating a computer in a computer". Not only is this a constructive proof of the Church-Turing thesis, but is also extremely common in all modern computers. For example, some programming languages use something called an interpreter, which is a simulated computer built on top of the basic computer; this allows programmers to write code (computer input) in a different language than the one understood by the base computer (the alternative is to use a compiler). Additionally, virtual machines are simulated computers which virtually replicate a physical computer in software, and are very commonly used by IT. Virtual machines are also a common technique used to create emulators, such game console emulators.

Artificial Intelligence

A computer will solve problems in exactly the way they are programmed to, without regard to efficiency nor alternative solutions nor possible shortcuts nor possible errors in the code. Computer programs which learn and adapt are part of the emerging field of artificial intelligence and machine learning.

Hardware

The term hardware covers all of those parts of a computer that are tangible objects. Circuits, displays, power supplies, cables, keyboards, printers and mice are all hardware.

History of computing hardware

First Generation (Mechanical/Electromechanical)	Calculators	Antikythera mechanism, Difference engine, Norden bombsight
	Programmable Devices	Jacquard loom, Analytical engine, Harvard Mark I, Z3
Second Generation (Vacuum Tubes)	Calculators	Atanasoff–Berry Computer, IBM 604, UNIVAC 60, UNIVAC 120
	Programmable Devices	Colossus, ENIAC, Manchester Small-Scale Experimental Machine, EDSAC, Manchester Mark 1, Ferranti Pegasus, Ferranti Mercury, CSIRAC, EDVAC, UNIVAC I, IBM 701, IBM 702, IBM 650, Z22
Third Generation (Discrete transistors and SSI, MSI, LSI Integrated circuits)	Mainframes	IBM 7090, IBM 7080, IBM System/360, BUNCH
	Minicomputer	PDP-8, PDP-11, IBM System/32, IBM System/36
	Minicomputer	VAX, IBM System i
	4-bit microcomputer	Intel 4004, Intel 4040
	8-bit microcomputer	Intel 8008, Intel 8080, Motorola 6800, Motorola 6809, MOS Technology 6502, Zilog Z80

Fourth Generation (VLSI integrated circuits)	16-bit microcomputer	Intel 8088, Zilog Z8000, WDC 65816/65802
	32-bit microcomputer	Intel 80386, Pentium, Motorola 68000, ARM architecture
	64-bit microcomputer[40]	Alpha, MIPS, PA-RISC, PowerPC, SPARC, x86-64
	Embedded computer	Intel 8048, Intel 8051
	Personal computer	Desktop computer, Home computer, Laptop computer, Personal digital assistant (PDA), Portable computer, Tablet PC, Wearable computer

Other Hardware Topics

Peripheral device (Input/output)	Input	Mouse, Keyboard, Joystick, Image scanner, Webcam, Graphics tablet, Microphone
	Output	Monitor, Printer, Loudspeaker
	Both	Floppy disk drive, Hard disk drive, Optical disc drive, Teleprinter
Computer busses	Short range	RS-232, SCSI, PCI, USB
	Long range (Computer networking)	Ethernet, ATM, FDDI

Software

Software refers to parts of the computer which do not have a material form, such as programs, data, protocols, etc. When software is stored in hardware that cannot easily be modified (such as BIOS ROM in an IBM PC compatible), it is sometimes called "firmware" to indicate that it falls into an uncertain area somewhere between hardware and software.

Computer software

Operating	Unix and BSD	UNIX System V, IBM AIX, HP-UX, Solaris (SunOS), IRIX, List of BSD operating systems
	GNU/Linux	List of Linux distributions, Comparison of Linux distributions
	Microsoft Windows	Windows 95, Windows 98, Windows NT, Windows 2000. Windows XP, Windows Vista, Windows 7

system	DOS	86-DOS (QDOS), PC-DOS, MS-DOS, DR-DOS, FreeDOS
	Mac OS	Mac OS classic, Mac OS X
	Embedded and real-time	List of embedded operating systems
	Experimental	Amoeba, Oberon/Bluebottle, Plan 9 from Bell Labs
	Multimedia	DirectX, OpenGL, OpenAL
Library	Programming library	C standard library, Standard Template Library
Data	Protocol	TCP/IP, Kermit, FTP, HTTP, SMTP
	File format	HTML, XML, JPEG, MPEG, PNG
User interface	Graphical user interface (WIMP)	Microsoft Windows, GNOME, KDE, QNX Photon, CDE, GEM, Aqua
	Text-based user interface	Command-line interface, Text user interface
Application	Office suite	Word processing, Desktop publishing, Presentation program, Database management system, Scheduling & Time management, Spreadsheet, Accounting software
	Internet Access	Browser, E-mail client, Web server, Mail transfer agent, Instant messaging
	Design and manufacturing	Computer-aided design, Computer-aided manufacturing, Plant management, Robotic manufacturing, Supply chain management
	Graphics	Raster graphics editor, Vector graphics editor, 3D modeler, Animation editor, 3D computer graphics, Video editing, Image processing
	Audio	Digital audio editor, Audio playback, Mixing, Audio synthesis, Computer music
	Software engineering	Compiler, Assembler, Interpreter, Debugger, Text editor, Integrated development environment, Software performance analysis, Revision control, Software configuration management
	Educational	Edutainment, Educational game, Serious game, Flight simulator

Programming Languages

Programming languages provide various ways of specifying programs for computers to run. Unlike natural languages, programming languages are designed to permit no ambiguity and to be concise. They are purely written languages and are often difficult to read aloud. They are generally either translated into machine code by a compiler or an assembler before being run, or translated directly at run time by an interpreter. Sometimes programs are executed by a hybrid method of the two techniques. There are thousands of different programming languages—some intended to be general purpose, others useful only for highly specialized applications.

Programming languages	
Lists of programming languages	Timeline of programming languages, List of programming languages by category, Generational list of programming languages, List of programming languages, Non-English-based programming languages
Commonly used Assembly languages	ARM, MIPS, x86
Commonly used high-level programming languages	Ada, BASIC, C, C++, C#, COBOL, Fortran, Java, Lisp, Pascal, Object Pascal
Commonly used Scripting languages	Bourne script, JavaScript, Python, Ruby, PHP, Perl

Professions and Organizations

As the use of computers has spread throughout society, there are an increasing number of careers involving computers.

Computer-related professions	
Hardware-related	Electrical engineering, Electronic engineering, Computer engineering, Telecommunications engineering, Optical engineering, Nanoengineering
Software-related	Computer science, Desktop publishing, Human–computer interaction, Information technology, Information systems, Computational science, Software engineering, Video game industry, Web design

The need for computers to work well together and to be able to exchange information has spawned the need for many standards organizations, clubs and societies of both a formal and informal nature.

Organizations	
Standards groups	ANSI, IEC, IEEE, IETF, ISO, W3C
Professional Societies	ACM, AIS, IET, IFIP, BCS
Free/Open source software groups	Free Software Foundation, Mozilla Foundation, Apache Software Foundation

E-learning

E-learning comprises all forms of electronically supported learning and teaching. The information and communication systems, whether networked or not, serve as specific media to implement the learning process. The term will still most likely be utilized to reference out-of-classroom and in-classroom educational experiences via technology, even as advances continue in regard to devices and curriculum.

E-learning is essentially the computer and network-enabled transfer of skills and knowledge. E-learning applications and processes include Web-based learning, computer-based learning, virtual classroom opportunities and digital collaboration. Content is delivered via the Internet, intranet/extranet, audio or video tape, satellite TV, and CD-ROM. It can be self-paced or instructor-led and includes media in the form of text, image, animation, streaming video and audio.

Abbreviations like CBT (*Computer-Based Training*), IBT (*Internet-Based Training*) or WBT (*Web-Based Training*) have been used as synonyms to e-learning. Today one can still find these terms being used, along with variations of e-learning such as elearning, Elearning, and eLearning. The terms will be utilized throughout this article to indicate their validity under the broader terminology of E-learning.

Computer Technology Concentration

This concentration provides the conceptual background and application skills needed to use computer technology. This concentration is not for technology managers, rather, managers who seek to add value to their organizational processes by understanding and integrating technology.

CECT 300 - Information Technology for Modern Organizations—Acquaints the student with the computer hardware and software resources required to function effectively in today's organizations. Students will also receive hands-on practice with software applications useful for organizational leadership. They will also examine the impact of the information highway on organizational operations.

CECT 410 - Databases as Productivity Tools—Explores the capabilities and basic architecture of a database and its role as an instrument of competitive advantage. The ability to operate and use a computer in the tasks of creation, retrieval and maintenance of data files will be covered. Through the use of hands-on tasks, case studies, and projects, students will apply the theories discussed to practical applications. Current microcomputer relational databases will be reviewed, and direct experience with one will be obtained (Microsoft Access). In addition, the ability to extract and organize data to better understand operational trends will be discussed.

CECT 425W - Electronic Communication and Cyberspace for the Leader—Introduces the world of electronic communications in a globally networked age. The student will be exposed to the vast array of online information resources available through the Internet. Additionally, the ability to communicate electronically in various mediums (text, sound, images) will be discussed. The areas covered will include the use of electronic communications in the developing arena of electronic data interchange and commerce, virtual private networks, intranets, and remote access to data. The use of electronic communications, such as security, privacy, backup, redundancy, and future trends will also be discussed.

CECT 450 - Network Operating Systems—Examines the workings of network operating systems (NOS) and examines the various services provided by an NOS including file services, application services, mail and messaging, distributed authentication and database functions. The major emphasis will be on the Windows NT and Unix operating systems, although Novell Network NDS and OS/2 will be discussed. Students completing this course should be able to evaluate various network operating systems in specific application contexts and provide justifications for the sizing and selection of a particular NOS including budgeting for capital and operating expenses.

CECT 470 - Multimedia Technology—Provides an overview of multimedia technology and its uses. Graphical User Interfaces, multimedia computer selections, scanners, sound digitizing, video and still cameras, CDROMs, multimedia and networking, multimedia and distance learning, digital video, graphics, sound and animation are examined. Students will create home pages on the World Wide Web as a means of integrating course concepts.

CECT 495W - Leadership Trends in Information Technology—This capstone course will investigate the use and application of technology into the business entity. Through case studies and best practice examples, students will analyze the synergism and advantages to be gained from successful implementations of technology. Current trends within the information technology industry and their relation to business success will be discussed. Students will produce a comprehensive case analysis to demonstrate their understanding and proficiency in the area of strategic application of information technologies.

4

Convention Management

Management in all business and organizational activities is the act of getting people together to accomplish desired goals and objectives using available resources efficiently and effectively. Management comprises planning, organizing, staffing, leading or directing, and controlling an organization (a group of one or more people or entities) or effort for the purpose of accomplishing a goal. Resourcing encompasses the deployment and manipulation of human resources, financial resources, technological resources, and natural resources.

Because organizations can be viewed as systems, management can also be defined as human action, including design, to facilitate the production of useful outcomes from a system. This view opens the opportunity to 'manage' oneself, a pre-requisite to attempting to manage others.

The verb *manage* comes from the Italian *maneggiare* (to handle — especially tools), which in turn derives from the Latin *manus* (hand). The French word *mesnagement* (later *ménagement*) influenced the development in meaning of the English word *management* in the 17th and 18th centuries.

Some definitions of management are:

1. Organization and coordination of the activities of an enterprise in accordance with certain policies and

in achievement of clearly defined objectives. Management is often included as a factor of production along with machines, materials, and money. According to the management guru Peter Drucker (1909–2005), the basic task of a management is twofold: marketing and innovation.

2. Directors and managers have the power and responsibility to make decisions to manage an enterprise. As a discipline, management comprises the interlocking functions of formulating corporate policy and organizing, planning, controlling, and directing the firm's resources to achieve the policy's objectives. The size of management can range from one person in a small firm to hundreds or thousands of managers in multinational companies. In large firms the board of directors formulates the policy which is implemented by the chief executive officer.

Theoretical Scope

At the beginning, one thinks of management functionally, as the action of measuring a quantity on a regular basis and of adjusting some initial plan; or as the actions taken to reach one's intended goal. This applies even in situations where planning does not take place. From this perspective, Frenchman Henri Fayol(1841–1925) considers management to consist of six functions:forecasting, planning, organizing, commanding, coordinating, controlling. He was one of the most influential contributors to modern concepts of management.

Another way of thinking, Mary Parker Follett (1868–1933), who wrote on the topic in the early twentieth century, defined management as "the art of getting things done through people". She described management as philosophy.

Some people, however, find this definition, while useful, far too narrow. The phrase "management is what managers do" occurs widely, suggesting the difficulty of defining management, the shifting nature of definitions, and the connection of managerial practices with the existence of a managerial cadre or class.

One habit of thought regards management as equivalent to "business administration" and thus excludes management in places outside commerce, as for example in charities and in the public sector. More realistically, however, every organization must manage its work, people, processes, technology, etc. in order to maximize its effectiveness. Nonetheless, many people refer to university departments which teach management as "business schools." Some institutions use that name while others employ the more inclusive term "management."

English speakers may also use the term "management" or "the management" as a collective word describing the managers of an organization, for example of a corporation. Historically this use of the term was often contrasted with the term "Labor" referring to those being managed.

Nature of Managerial Work

In for-profit work, management has as its primary function the satisfaction of a range of stakeholders. This typically involves making a profit (for the shareholders), creating valued products at a reasonable cost (for customers), and providing rewarding employment opportunities (for employees). In nonprofit management, add the importance of keeping the faith of donors. In most models of management/governance, shareholders vote for the board of directors, and the board then hires senior management. Some organizations have experimented with other methods (such as employee-voting models) of selecting or reviewing managers; but this occurs only very rarely.

In the public sector of countries constituted as representative democracies, voters elect politicians to public office. Such politicians hire many managers and administrators, and in some countries like the United States political appointees lose their jobs on the election of a new president/governor/mayor.

Historical Development

Difficulties arise in tracing the history of management. Some see it (by definition) as a late modern (in the sense of late modernity) conceptualization. On those terms it cannot have a pre-modern history, only harbingers (such as stewards). Others, however, detect management-like-thought back to Sumerian traders and to the builders of the pyramids of ancient Egypt. Slave-owners through the centuries faced the problems of exploiting/motivating a dependent but sometimes unenthusiastic or recalcitrant workforce, but many pre-industrial enterprises, given their small scale, did not feel compelled to face the issues of management systematically. However, innovations such as the spread of Arabic numerals (5th to 15th centuries) and the codification of double-entry book-keeping (1494) provided tools for management assessment, planning and control.

Given the scale of most commercial operations and the lack of mechanized record-keeping and recording before the industrial revolution, it made sense for most owners of enterprises in those times to carry out management functions by and for themselves. But with growing size and complexity of organizations, the split between owners (individuals, industrial dynasties or groups of shareholders) and day-to-day managers (independent specialists in planning and control) gradually became more common.

Early Writing

While management has been present for millennia, several writers have created a background of works that assisted in modern management theories.

Sun Tzu's The Art of War

Written by Chinese general Sun Tzu in the 6th century BC, *The Art of War* is a military strategy book that, for managerial purposes, recommends being aware of and acting on strengths and weaknesses of both a manager's organization and a foe's.

Chanakya's Arthashastra

Chanakya wrote the Arthashastra around 300BC in which various stategies, techniques and management theories were written which gives an account on the management of empires, economy and family. The work is often compared to the later works of Machiavelli.

Niccolò Machiavelli's The Prince

Believing that people were motivated by self-interest, Niccolò Machiavelli wrote *The Prince* in 1513 as advice for the city of Florence, Italy. Machiavelli recommended that leaders use fear—but not hatred—to maintain control.

Adam Smith's The Wealth of Nations

Written in 1776 by Adam Smith, a Scottish moral philosopher, *The Wealth of Nations* aims for efficient organization of work through Specialization of labor. Smith described how changes in processes could boost productivity in the manufacture of pins. While individuals could produce 200 pins per day, Smith analyzed the steps involved in manufacture and, with 10 specialists, enabled production of 48,000 pins per day.

19th Century

Classical economists such as Adam Smith (1723–1790) and John Stuart Mill (1806–1873) provided a theoretical background to resource-allocation, production, and pricing issues. About the same time, innovators like Eli Whitney (1765–1825), James Watt (1736–1819), and Matthew Boulton (1728–1809) developed elements of technical production such as standardization, quality-control procedures, cost-accounting, interchangeability of parts, and work-planning. Many of these aspects of management existed in the pre-1861 slave-based sector of the US economy. That environment saw 4 million people, as the contemporary usages had it, "managed" in profitable quasi-mass production.

By the late 19th century, marginal economists Alfred Marshall (1842–1924), Léon Walras (1834–1910), and others introduced a new layer of complexity to the theoretical underpinnings of management. Joseph Wharton offered the first tertiary-level course in management in 1881.

20th Century

By about 1900 one finds managers trying to place their theories on what they regarded as a thoroughly scientific basis. Examples include Henry R. Towne's *Science of management* in the 1890s, Frederick Winslow Taylor's *The Principles of Scientific Management* (1911), Frank and Lillian Gilbreth's *Applied motion study* (1917), and Henry L. Gantt's charts (1910s). J. Duncan wrote the first college management textbook in 1911. In 1912 Yoichi Ueno introduced Taylorism to Japan and became first management consultant of the "Japanese-management style". His son Ichiro Ueno pioneered Japanese quality assurance.

The first comprehensive theories of management appeared around 1920. The Harvard Business School invented the Master of Business Administration degree (MBA) in 1921. People like Henri Fayol (1841–1925) and Alexander Church described the various branches of management and their inter-relationships. In the early 20th century, people like Ordway Tead (1891–1973), Walter Scott and J. Mooney applied the principles of psychology to management, while other writers, such as Elton Mayo (1880–1949), Mary Parker Follett (1868–1933), Chester Barnard (1886–1961), Max Weber (1864–1920), Rensis Likert (1903–1981), and Chris Argyris (1923 -) approached the phenomenon of management from a sociological perspective.

Peter Drucker (1909–2005) wrote one of the earliest books on applied management: *Concept of the Corporation* (published in 1946). It resulted from Alfred Sloan (chairman of General Motors until 1956) commissioning a study of the organisation. Drucker went on to write 39 books, many in the same vein.

H. Dodge, Ronald Fisher (1890–1962), and Thornton C. Fry introduced statistical techniques into management-studies. In the 1940s, Patrick Blackett combined these statistical theories with microeconomic theory and gave birth to the science of operations research. Operations research, sometimes known as "management science" (but distinct from Taylor's scientific management), attempts to take a scientific approach to solving management problems, particularly in the areas of logistics and operations.

Some of the more recent developments include the Theory of Constraints, management by objectives, reengineering, Six Sigma and various information-technology-driven theories such as agile software development, as well as group management theories such as Cog's Ladder.

As the general recognition of managers as a class solidified during the 20th century and gave perceived practitioners of the art/science of management a certain amount of prestige, so the way opened for popularised systems of management ideas to peddle their wares. In this context many management fads may have had more to do with pop psychology than with scientific theories of management.

Towards the end of the 20th century, business management came to consist of six separate branches, namely:

1. Human resource management
2. Operations management or production management
3. Strategic management
4. Marketing management
5. Financial management
6. Information technology management responsible for management information systems

21st Century

In the 21st century observers find it increasingly difficult to subdivide management into functional categories in this way. More and more processes simultaneously involve several categories. Instead, one tends to think in terms of the various processes, tasks, and objects subject to management.

Branches of management theory also exist relating to nonprofits and to government: such as public administration, public management, and educational management. Further, management programs related to civil-society organizations have also spawned programs in nonprofit management and social entrepreneurship.

Note that many of the assumptions made by management have come under attack from business ethics viewpoints, critical management studies, and anti-corporate activism.

As one consequence, workplace democracy has become both more common, and more advocated, in some places distributing all management functions among the workers, each of whom takes on a portion of the work. However, these models predate any current political issue, and may occur more naturally than does a command hierarchy. All management to some degree embraces democratic principles in that in the long term workers must give majority support to management; otherwise they leave to find other work, or go on strike. Despite the move toward workplace democracy, command-and-control organization structures remain commonplace and the *de facto* organization structure. Indeed, the entrenched nature of command-and-control can be seen in the way that recent layoffs have been conducted with management ranks affected far less than employees at the lower levels of organizations. In some cases, management has even rewarded itself with bonuses when lower level employees have been laid off.

Basic Functions/Roles

Management operates through various functions, often classified as planning, organizing, staffing, leading/ directing, and controlling/monitoring.i.e

Planning: Deciding what needs to happen in the future (today, next week, next month, next year, over the next 5 years, etc.) and generating plans for action.

Organizing: (Implementation) making optimum use of the resources required to enable the successful carrying out of plans.

Staffing: Job Analyzing, recruitment, and hiring individuals for appropriate jobs.

Leading/Directing: Determining what needs to be done in a situation and getting people to do it.

Controlling/Monitoring: Checking progress against plans.

Motivation : Motivation is also a kind of basic function of management, because without motivation, employees cannot work effectively. If motivation doesn't take place in an organization, then employees may not contribute to the other functions (which are usually set by top level management).

Formation of the Business Policy

1. The **mission** of the business is the most obvious purpose—which may be, for example, to make soap.
2. The **vision** of the business reflects its aspirations and specifies its intended direction or future destination.
3. The **objectives** of the business refers to the ends or activity at which a certain task is aimed.
4. The business's **policy** is a guide that stipulates rules, regulations and objectives, and may be used in the managers' decision-making. It must be flexible and easily interpreted and understood by all employees.
5. The business's **strategy** refers to the coordinated plan of action that it is going to take, as well as the resources that it will use, to realize its vision and long-term objectives. It is a guideline to managers, stipulating how they ought to allocate and utilize

the factors of production to the business's advantage. Initially, it could help the managers decide on what type of business they want to form.

Implementation of Policies and Strategies

1. All policies and strategies must be discussed with all managerial personnel and staff.
2. Managers must understand where and how they can implement their policies and strategies.
3. A plan of action must be devised for each department.
4. Policies and strategies must be reviewed regularly.
5. Contingency plans must be devised in case the environment changes.
6. Assessments of progress ought to be carried out regularly by top-level managers.
7. A good environment and team spirit is required within the business.
8. The missions, objectives, strengths and weaknesses of each department must be analysed to determine their roles in achieving the business's mission.
9. The **forecasting method** develops a reliable picture of the business's future environment.
10. A **planning unit** must be created to ensure that all plans are consistent and that policies and strategies are aimed at achieving the same mission and objectives.

    All policies must be discussed with all managerial personnel and staff that is required in the execution of any departmental policy.
11. Organizational change is strategically achieved through the implementation of the eight-step plan

of action established by John P. Kotter: Increase urgency, get the vision right, communicate the buy-in, empower action, create short-term wins, don't let up, and make change stick.

Policies and Strategies in the Planning Process

1. They give mid- and lower-level managers a good idea of the future plans for each department in an organization.
2. A framework is created whereby plans and decisions are made.
3. Mid- and lower-level management may add their own plans to the business's strategic ones.

Multi-divisional Hierarchy

The management of a large organization may have about five levels:

1. Senior management (or "top management" or "upper management")
2. Middle management
3. Low-level management, such as supervisors or team-leaders
4. Foreman
5. Rank and File

Top-level Management

1. Require an extensive knowledge of management roles and skills.
2. They have to be very aware of external factors such as markets.
3. Their decisions are generally of a long-term nature

4. Their decisions are made using analytic, directive, conceptual and/or behavioral/participative processes
5. They are responsible for **strategic** decisions.
6. They have to chalk out the plan and see that plan may be effective in the future.
7. They are executive in nature.

Middle Management

1. Mid-level managers have a specialized understanding of certain managerial tasks.
2. They are responsible for carrying out the decisions made by top-level management.
3. finance,marketing etc comes under middle level management

Lower Management

1. This level of management ensures that the decisions and plans taken by the other two are carried out.
2. Lower-level managers' decisions are generally short-term ones.

Foreman / lead Hand

1. They are people who have direct supervision over the working force in office, factory, sales field, or other workgroup or area of activity.

Rank and File

1. The responsibilities of the persons belonging to this group are even more restricted and more specific than those of the foreman.

Hotel Management Courses

The boom in the tourism industry has resulted in the immense growth of hotel industry in India. The hotel industry promises a bright future for anyone who wishes to take up a career in this segment. The students opting for hotel management career courses must have an affinity towards socializing and understanding the needs of the people.

As hotels fall under the service industry, the motive of hotel management courses in India is to prepare the students to face the challenges of this competitive world. As far as tourism industry in India is concerned, it is attracting tourists from across the world and this definitely calls for quality hospitality.

Hotel Management as a Career Option

Hotel management is one of the most interesting career options in the contemporary job market. Career training from a recognized and reputed hotel management institute is just an icing on the cake.

In India there are many hotel management institutes and colleges which provide hospitality or hotel management courses.

These hotel management courses make one aware of the operating-sections of the hotel industry like front office, general operations, sales and marketing, food and beverage, service keeping and catering.

Hotel Management Course Admissions

Candidates seeking admission to the hotel management courses in India need to pass their 12th standard examination with English as a subject. Students with a bachelor's degree from any recognized university may also join some of the management training schemes offered by various institutions. Admission depends on the performance of the students in the written admission test, personal interview round and group discussion session. The time duration of the courses offered by several institutes may vary from six months to three years.

Hotel Management Course Scope

Hotel management job opportunities exists both in the private and public sector. One can look for various openings available in the hotels of the nation. Most of the hotels in India offer lucrative pay packages to the suitable candidates. The jobs offered are satisfying as well as highly rewarding.

Professional Convention Management Association

The Professional Convention Management Association (PCMA) is the leading organization for meetings and event professionals. Its mission is to deliver superior and innovative education and promote the value of professional convention management.

Members

PCMA represents nearly 6,000 meetings industry leaders including planner professionals, suppliers, faculty and students. Members are categorized as either professionals or suppliers depending on their job function.

1. **Professionals**: individuals who are responsible for the development, organization, and management of meetings, conventions, exhibits, and seminars. PCMA professional members represent meeting, conference and convention planners; exhibit managers; and independent meeting planners from corporations and associations.

2. **Suppliers**: individuals whose organization is engaged in providing products and services related to the conduct and operation of meetings, conventions, exhibits, and seminars. PCMA supplier members represent all aspects of the hospitality industry including destinations, convention and visitor bureaus (CVBs), convention centers, hotels, transportation, audio visual and service providers.

Education

PCMA provides top-level education through innovative experiential learning sessions, extraordinary networking opportunities, and high-level discussions on the industry's most challenging issues. Programs include the Annual Meeting, Executive Edge, The Masters Series, "On-the-Go!" Webinars, CMP Online Prep and much more.

History

PCMA began in 1956 with its first Annual Meeting held in Philadelphia and incorporated as an organization shortly after in 1957. Initially, PCMA was designed to be a networking association for health care association executives. Throughout the years, PCMA's initial focus shifted to providing both networking and educational opportunities for meeting professionals at all levels, plus suppliers, faculty and students. Currently, PCMA represents nearly 6,000 members from 16 chapters in the United States and Canada.

PCMA has published *Convene*; magazine since 1986. *Convene* is one of the meeting industry's premier monthly magazines and provides in-depth information on all aspects of meeting management to more than 30,000 subscribers. Convene is the recipient of numerous awards, including the 2003 EXCEL Society of National Association Publications

Gold Award. PCMA's current president and CEO is Deborah Sexton, a 30-year veteran of the meetings and convention industry. Prior to joining PCMA in March 2005, she served as President of the Chicago Convention and Tourism Bureau. Sexton is also president of PCMA's Education Foundation.

Education Foundation

The role of the PCMA Education Foundation is to support the mission of PCMA through fundraising and grant giving focused on education and research that will benefit the meetings and convention industry.

In 1985, PCMA established the PCMA Education Foundation. The role of the Foundation is to support educational programs to improve professionalism in the meetings industry and to provide university-level meeting management curriculum through fundraising and grant giving. Each year, a new Board of Trustees is elected to lead the Foundation and is supported by the work of committees and task forces. Four fundraising events are held by the Foundation each year; these events are: Dinner Celebrating Professional Achievement, The PCMA Education Foundation Partnership Summit, Party With a Purpose, and The Silent Auction. These events allow the Foundation to fund student scholarships, provide grants for meetings industry research and education initiatives, and fund communities in need.

Since 1956, PCMA's signature educational event has been its Annual Meeting. Over the years, attendance has grown from six in 1956 to more than 3,000 in 2008. The meeting takes place each January and features numerous educational sessions and networking opportunities. Education sessions are designed to deliver new strategies and innovative solutions to attendees. In 2006, PCMA celebrated its 50th Annual Meeting in Philadelphia. Future locations include New Orleans in 2009 and Dallas in 2010..

Convention Center

A convention center (American English, conference centre British English) is a large building that is designed to hold a convention, where individuals and groups gather to promote and share common interests. Convention centers typically offer sufficient floor area to accommodate several thousand attendees. Very large venues, suitable for major trade shows, are sometimes known as 'exhibition centres'. Convention centers typically have at least one auditorium and may also contain concert halls, lecture halls, meeting rooms, and conference rooms. Some large resort area hotels include a convention center.

5

Convention Planning

Convention planning is the process of planning a festival, ceremony, competition, party, or convention. Event planning includes budgeting, establishing dates and alternate dates, selecting and reserving the event site, acquiring permits, and coordinating transportation and parking. Event planning also includes some or all of the following, depending on the event: developing a theme or motif for the event, arranging for speakers and alternate speakers, coordinating location support (such as electricity and other utilities), arranging decor, tables, chairs, tents, event support and security, catering, police, fire, portable toilets, parking, signage, emergency plans, health care professionals, and cleanup.

Steps to Planning an Event/Convention

The first step to planning an event is determining its purpose, whether it is for a wedding, company, birthday, festival, graduation or any other event requiring extensive planning. From this the event planner needs to choose entertainment, location, guest list, speakers, and content. The location for events is endless, but with event planning they would likely be held at hotels, convention centers, reception halls, or outdoors depending on the event. Once the location is set the coordinator/planner needs to prepare the event with staff, set up the entertainment, and keep contact with the client. After all this is set the event planner has all the smaller details to address like set up of the event such as food, drinks, music, guest list, budget, advertising and marketing, decorations, all this preparation is what is needed for an event to run smoothly. An event planner needs to be able to manage their time wisely for the event, and the length of preparation needed for each event so it is a success.

Event Planning as a Career

Event planning is a relatively new career field. There is now training that helps one trying to break into the career field. There must be training for an event planner to handle all the pressure and work efficiently. This career deals with a lot of communication and organization aspects. There are many different names for an event planner such as a conference coordinator, a convention planner, a special event coordinator, and a meeting manager.

Event planners' work is considered either stressful or energizing. This line of work is also considered fast paced and demanding. Planners face deadlines and communicating with multiple people at one time. Planners spend most of their time in offices, but when meeting with clients the work is usually on-site at the location where the event is taking place . Some physical activity is required such as carrying boxes of materials and decorations or supplies needed for the event. Also, long working hours can be a part of the job. The day the event is taking place could start as early as 5:00 a.m. and then work until midnight. Working on weekends is sometimes required, which is when many events take place .

How to Plan a Convention Display

Often, the best way to get noticed, get exposure and get readers is to actually put yourself in the path of those who are looking for your brand of entertainment. Applying for a table at the next comics convention and showing up with a few books and fliers isn't enough. In order to catch a convention-goer's eye you need an attractive display that will help you stand out from all the other tables in the room. These basics will work no matter what size your booth or the type of product you are selling.

Instructions

Know how much space you have to work with. A table is different from a booth, but only in how you arrange your elements. The important things to know are how big your table (or part of one) will be and whether you have additional floor space for traffic flow or just enough for your chair.

Identify yourself with eye-catching signs and banners. Order at least two banners: one to hang from the front of your table and one to hang or stand behind you. Whether it hangs from posts above your head at the back of the booth or has its own stand, just make sure it's at or just above eye-level. If money is tight, but skill and time are available, consider painting your own banners directly onto a piece of canvas.

Drape the table in a colorful cloth. As most cons are held in hotels or convention centers it's usual to have each table covered and skirted to provide a professional, if uniform look. In order to attract a buyer's eye you must stand out from the crowd, and a simple cloth, plain or patterned, will help do that as well as theme your few square feet of space. A separate cloth also gives you the chance to pre-install the hanging hardware for your table banner.

Set out plenty of merchandise. Scarcity actually works against you when trying to sell books, prints or anything else; an abundance of product will invite guests to browse. Stack your books high and use some sort of stand to set at least one book upright. Prints or portfolios can be propped up on a stand to encourage browsers to flip through without having to bend over your table.

Encourage interaction by having something for the attendees to do at your booth. A game or drawing, trivia contests or a do-it-yourself project are all good ideas for this. Even if you just work on your craft during slower times, stay near the action and look up frequently to engage any curious onlookers. Consider posting a sign that says: "feel free to ask questions" or narrate your process as you work when people arrive.

Publications and Resources

Many business-to-business trade publications exist to help event planning and production professionals become educated about the issues and trends in their industry. Many are controlled circulation publications available at no cost to qualified event professionals. Qualification is based on multiple variables like job title, company type, industry segment or geographic region, and is at the publisher's discretion.

How to Plan a Conference and Convention

The conference and convention industry in the United States is a $175 billion a year behemoth, according to travel researcher PhoCusWright. The role of conference and convention planner has become a popular, respected profession. There are now between 50,000 and 75,000 conference and meeting planners in the U.S., according to industry estimates. Major industry organizations include

Meeting Professionals International, the Professional Convention Management Association and the Convention Industry Council.

Instructions

Decide whether the event is being staged for profit or as an internal business function of your company or organization. For example, trade associations and private-sector conference production companies typically do conferences and conventions for profit. Most businesses and government entities do them as private events, such as sales conferences or training seminars, and pay the travel expenses of attendees.

Create a detailed business plan. Negotiate written contracts with all vendors, such as a hotel, bus company or restaurant. If your event is for profit, you will make money on the difference between what you pay for the hotel room or meal, versus what attendees pay you. Look for creative ways to make money, such as selling DVDs or podcasts of important seminars or training sessions.

Establish a comprehensive operating budget. Project the number of attendees you will attract and multiply that by your planned event registration fee. Add the projected profit from the sale of hotel rooms, meals and other activities to attendees. The combined number is your total projected revenue. Subtract your total costs and you will have a profit target.

Select an alluring destination. The draw of the destination will be one of the most important factors in the success of any conference or convention. It's no accident that the top convention destinations in the U.S. include Las Vegas, New Orleans and Orlando — unique cities with a range of dining and entertainment options.

Select a headquarters hotel. Although attendees can make their own reservations and stay elsewhere, the headquarters hotel will be the focal point of the conference or convention. It's where general sessions and breakout meetings will be held each day, as well as social events in the evening.

Negotiate hotel meeting and event space at a reduced cost — or for free. For a conference involving several hundred room nights or more, most major hotels will give away the meeting space in return for a guarantee of a minimum amount of food-and-beverage business, including snacks and refreshments on the breaks during the day. Most hotels use a free meeting space to total room night ratio, so the more room nights you're generating, the better the deal you can negotiate. If you need the local convention center, it is usually provided at minimal or no cost, provided you meet a minimum number of hotel room nights.

Meeting and Convention Planner

A meeting and convention planner supervises and coordinates the strategic, operational and logistical activities necessary for the production of events. The planner can be employed or hired ad hoc by corporations, associations, governments, and other organizations.

Standardization Issues

1. Although the Occupational Information Network (O*NET), sponsored by the United States Department of Labor and Employment and Training Administration, identified this occupation as "meeting and convention planner," other titles are more commonly used. These titles include *event planner, meeting planner,* and *meeting manager*. In addition, a number of other titles specific to the

categories of events produced are used, such as *corporate planner* and *party planner*.

2. The *banquet event order* (BEO), a standard form used in the hospitality industry to document the requirements of an event as pertinent to the venue, has presented numerous problems to meeting and convention planners due to the increasing complexity and scope of modern events. In response, Convention Industry Council developed the *event specifications guide* (ESG) that is currently replacing the BEO.
3. Additionally, the Convention Industry Council is spearheading The Accepted Practices Exchange (APEX). By bringing planners and suppliers together to create industry-wide accepted practices and a common terminology, the profession continues to enhance the professionalism of the meetings, conventions and exhibitions industry.

Programs

Certification	Acronym	Issuing Organization
Certified Association Executive	CAE	American Society of Association Executives
Certified Destination Management Executive	CDME	International Association of Convention and Visitors Bureaus
Certified in Exhibition Management	CEM	International Association for Exhibition Management
Certified Event Rental Professional	CERP	American Rental Association
Certified Festival Executive	CFE	International Festivals and Events Association
Certified Hospitality Marketing Executive	CHME	Hospitality Sales and Marketing Association International
Certified Incentive Travel Executive	CITE	Society of Incentive and Travel Executives
Certified Meeting Professional	CMP	Convention Industry Council
Global Certification in Meeting Management	CMM	Meeting Professionals International
Certified Professional Catering Executive	CPCE	National Association of Catering Executives

Certified Special Events Professional	CSEP	International Special Events Society
Destination Management Certified Professional	DMCP	Association of Destination Management Executives
Professional Bridal Consultant	PBC	Association of Bridal Consultants

MEETING PROFESSIONALS INTERNATIONAL

Meeting Professionals International (MPI) is a professional community for the global meetings industry. Founded in 1972, the Dallas-based non-profit association has 68 chapters and clubs, over 24,000 members from 69 chapters in 20 countries around the world. It organizes four annual conferences: the World Education Congress (summer), the MeetDifferent (winter), the Asian Meetings and Event Conference (fall), and the European Meeting and Events Conference (spring). MPI publishes ***One+ Magazine*** (formerly The Meeting Professional) with online access to selected articles. One+ is mailed monthly to MPI members as a member benefit.

Certified Meeting Professional (CMP) Program

An accredited designation offered by the Convention Industry Council; this designation certifies competency in 27 areas of meeting management through application and examination.

Certification in Meeting Management (CMM)

Certification program offered by Meeting Professionals International. Global certification in meeting management that focuses on strategic thinking and actions for senior-level meeting professionals.

Culture Active Tool

The MPI CultureActive Tool is an added component of MPI Member Solutions that offers MPI members the opportunity to improve their ability to understand and communicate with other cultures – improving cultural competence and acquisition of skills.

Global Certificate in Meeting Operations (GCMO).

Global Certificate in Meeting Operations I

For those who are relatively new to the industry (less than 3 years), MPI will offer the Global Certificate in Meeting Operations I (GCMO). This certificate, based on an internationally consistent Body of Knowledge and therefore easily transferable, was created from the re-imagined Institutes I.

Global Certificate in Meeting Operations II

For those who possess more industry experience, MPI will offer the Global Certificate in Meeting Operations II (GCMO). This certificate, based on an internationally consistent Body of Knowledge and therefore easily transferable, will be created from the re-imagined Institutes I and possibly II and III.

Global Certificate in Meeting Operations III

For those who are at an intermediate-to-advance level in their career, but beyond the CMP level, MPI will offer a second Global Certificate in Meeting Operations (CMO). This certificate will be created from the re-imagined Institutes III, or parts of II as appropriate.

Executive Leadership Program

For the most senior and executive level industry professionals who have progressed beyond the need for meeting and event management education, MPI has plans to develop a leadership program (e.g., MBA level, focused on business executive leadership skills) for presentation at its conferences or as a stand-alone opportunity, along with opportunities for on-going engagement between members of this community.

MPI Chapter

MPI Chapters provide an education and networking link between members in a specific locality.

Digital Content Resource Center (DCRC)

The MPI Digital Content Resource Center (DCRC) strives to provide searchable content that shapes an educational experience for members. As new content is generated through live events, digital connections, strategic partnerships, etc. the life of the content will be provided here as a value added service.

Virtual Knowledge Center

CSR Webinar Series

MPI presents a series webinars on corporate social responsibility as a free benefit of membership.

Harvard & Kiplinger Webinar Series

CMP Online Study Guide

A focused and flexible program designed to support preparation for the CMP exam.

Corporate Social Responsibility (CSR)

MPI provides publications and seminars on Corporate Social Responsibility, a businesses' need to address its sustainability and impact on society in addition to profits. This is known as the triple bottom line.

Meeting Industry Wiki

MPI's own wiki of meeting industry terms and related articles.

Professional Pathways

MPI Professional Pathways is a suite of online personalized products and services to meet the career growth and resource needs of meeting professionals. It includes My Skills Assessment, My Gap Report and My Skills Assessment Recommended Resources.

Ceu's

MPI provides Continuing Education Unit (CEU) credits for learning activities as an additional membership benefit.

MPI Scholarships

CATEGORY I – College Education Funding is money designated for college work towards undergraduate or graduate degrees and requires acceptance in a program of study. CATEGORY II - General Leadership Education or Academic Funding is money designated for knowledge/education sought inside or outside the traditional academic institution. CATEGORY III – MPI Programs is money designated specifically for leadership, career and educational opportunities offered exclusively by MPI itself.

Universities

MPI offers lists of Universities with Hospitality or Meeting and Events courses of study.

MPI Global Marketplace

Resources for meeting and event suppliers.

MPI Foundation

The MPI Foundation powers the vision of Meeting Professionals International (MPI). Contributions from MPI members, chapters, and organizations are invested in high-impact programs to support a rich, global meetings and events industry and provide investment into the future of the meetings and events profession.

MPI Bookstore

The MPI Bookstore contains a large catalog of materials including CD-ROMs, books, e-books, templates and reports, and MPI logo materials. These resources, many available at a reduced cost, are provided as a benefit to MPI members.

Emec

The European Meetings and Events Conference, co-created by Meeting Professionals International (MPI), brings together industry professionals from all over Europe and around the world for three days of education and next-level networking.

Gmec

Meeting Professionals International (MPI) will host its second annual Gulf Meetings and Events Conference in Abu Dhabi in March 2009, in an effort to continue building a vibrant community for meeting and event professionals in the Gulf region.

Meet Different

The event, usually held every February (formerly Professional Education Conference - North America or PEC-NA), is the first meeting industry conference where the organizers are creating new session ideas and formats. The extensive use of wikis and blogs and social networking complements the new format, and is attempting to help industry professionals better understand and use the new tools available to them.

World Education Congress (WEC)

The World Education Congress is MPI's global conference that is held annually in July or August, traditionally somewhere in North America. The WEC features education sessions with a focus on business, leadership and other career-development skills. There is a tradeshow component (MeetingPlace). WEC has a more international perspective than does MPI's other conferences. It also offers General Sessions and networking and marketplace/business opportunities.

Event Scheduling

Event scheduling is the activity of finding a suitable time for an event such as meeting, conference, trip, etc. It is an important part of event planning that is usually carried out at its beginning stage. In general, event scheduling must take into account what impact particular dates of the event could have on the success of the event. When organizing a scientific conference, for example, organizers might take into account the knowledge in which periods classes are held at universities, since it is expected that many potential participants are university professors. They should also try to check that no other similar conferences are held at the same time, because overlapping would make a problem for those participants who are interesting in attending all conferences.

When it is well known who is expected to attend the event (e.g. in the case of a project meeting), organizers usually try to synchronize the time of the event with planned schedules of all participants. This is a difficult task when there are many participants or when the participants are located at distant places. In such cases, the organizers should first define a set of suggested dates and address a query about suitable dates to potential participants. After response is obtained from all participants, the event time suitable for most of participants is selected. This procedure can be alleviated by internet tools.

6

Hotel Convention Sales

Today, it would be considered an unwise business practice to plan an event without a contract for the facilities and each service to be utilized. Not so long ago contracts of this type were only one or two pages in length and usually written by the director of sales. The art of negotiation has always been an important skill to master, but it became much more of a challenge as revenue management entered our vocabulary. In this article we will examine all of these important subjects, and review some samples of current contracts in use.

Procedures

As discussed in last article, the initial contact or inquiry is made between the facility (hotel) sales department and the group planner. The negotiation may begin at that time or commence after collateral information has been exchanged: a sales kit, Web site, or whatever.

We will examine the general order of correspondence that leads up to a contract. Keep in mind that hotels have seen the lead time (when the initial inquiry is made) for corporate meetings dramatically reduced in recent years. Seven to nine months in advance is now more like two to four months, or even less. The association market, on the other hand, hasn't deviated from its standard annual convention pattern:

1. Proposal Letter
2. Letter of Agreement
3. Contract

If the lead time is short, the proposal letter and letter of agreement might be combined into one document. In that case, the following information would be included:

1. Dates for which hotel rooms will be held
2. Dates for which meeting function space will be held
3. Room rates for each room type to be held
4. All arrangements negotiated and agreed to and date of expiration on offer extended
5. Signature may be optional
6. Yield or revenue management

Regardless of whether these two documents are combined, it is essential that all arrangements are listed and restated as agreed. This protects both the client and the facility and alleviates any potential misunderstandings. All changes and amendments to the proposal normally are written in here and then initialed by both parties. Unfortunately, verbal agreements or handshakes are not practical, as people often will recall words differently when memory fades.

Other Forms of A Proposal

A request for a proposal (RFP) is a fairly new document that quickly has become an industry standard utilized by hotels companies. The RFP can usually be found on its Web site, under Groups, "Plan a Meeting" or similar menu tab. It is often promoted as a tool to make the inquiry for meeting and hotel room space much easier for the group planner.

The typical request for a proposal includes much of the same information as a proposal letter, with an expected faster response to the electronic inquiry. It should be noted that prior to that development many large associations and organizations with multiple meetings and annual conventions had RFPs.

They were sent to all sites under consideration. The DMAI or IACVB (International Association of Convention and Visitors Bureaus) has developed a comprehensive database of RFPs that lists group requirements that are available to all member convention and visitor bureaus.

Checking out the Online Site

Selection and Rfps Options

Throw out the meeting facility guides and dusty stacks of hotel brochures. Forget about faxing or express mailing your RFPs (requests for proposals) to many individual hotels. These inefficient paper-based means of finding and booking meeting facilities are falling way to web-based products that provide richer detail in faster, more convenient, and, sometimes, completely new ways.

The first online RFP site appeared in January 1996 with the Radisson Miyako Hotel San Francisco, offering a simple online meeting space request form. In four short years, a plethora of Web sites have sprung up offering everything from extensive, searchable meeting facility databases, automated RFP forms that can be sent to multiple facilities with a click, Hot Dates, and, most recently, online auctions. These sites vary considerably in the size of their databases, the richness of meeting facility detail, and how they generate revenue.

This article will help sort them out. It includes all of the major and some of the minor sites with detailed information regarding database size/usefulness, pricing models and special features, to help choose which will be the best one(s) for you.

Contracts

In many cases one or both of the original parties who drew up the agreement may no longer be employed by those companies. Job turnover in the hotel industry is very high. Remember also that large associations must book their conventions up to five or eight years in advance. These and other concerns—especially failure to perform—necessitate that the contract be written with legal guidance.

Today, all hotel and convention facilities have legal departments that do just that. In recent years the numbers of lawsuits brought by hotels against groups that fail to fully utilize their room block has escalated. This is known as attrition (more on this subject later in this article). Therefore, experts recommend today that contract language and contents be standardized throughout the organization. The four required elements are:

1. The offer
2. The acceptance
3. The obligation
4. The consideration (usually monetary)

The following subjects areas or sections should be addressed and spelled out in complete detail:

1. Name of the organization and hotel
2. Dates hotel rooms are being held
3. Dates meeting/function space is being held
4. Room rates for each room type being held (room block)
5. Number of each type of room being held (room block)

6. Date room block will be released (rate no longer available)
7. All meeting and function space being held
8. Scheduled food and beverage functions and guarantees with required time notification and amount percent of food to be prepared over guarantee
9. Names of representatives from the organization and hotel (their signatures required)
10. Complimentary room arrangements ratio agreed to, or any discounts
11. Reservations procedures
12. Exhibit space registration policies
13. Attrition clauses or penalties
14. All arrangements negotiated and agreed to and date of expiration on offer extended

Differences Between A Tentative Proposal and A Final Contract

The initial requirements will be itemized in the tentative proposal. All negotiated written and verbal amendments agreed to by the parties will now be drawn up into a new document—a contract. The final contract will have language predetermined by the legal department, which clearly spells out the enforceable obligations required by each party. In the contract all additional changes are initialed and signed. Figure 7.3 is a sample of a hotel group contract, with sections that cover many key negotiated areas of concern to both buyer and seller.

Room Blocks

The CIC defined a block as (1) the total number of sleeping rooms reserved for an event, (2) the number of rooms, seats, or space reserved in advance for a group, and (3) to assign space. The room pickup is defined as the number of facility guest rooms actually used out of a room block. The group room block commitment is included as part of the final contract. This section of the form should always include the following:

1. Dates the meeting function space is being held
2. Room rates for each room type being held (room block)
3. Number of each type of room being held (room block)
4. Date the room block will be released (rate no longer available)
5. Penalties, fees resulting from unused rooms in block—not released
6. Sliding scale of charges applicable for each time period block not utilized

Decades ago, hotels began to make meeting room rental fees directly tied to the number of guest (sleeping) rooms utilized by the group hotel. Both large and small meeting convention groups agreed to this method, primarily because they did not want to pay for meeting space rental. However, years ago, when attendees began to book "outside the room block" (for a variety of reasons—see following) and stay at less expensive properties, failure to fulfill contractual obligations began.

Throughout this article and in articles in the appendixes, many examples of effective strategies for this issue have also been provided for your consideration.

Negotiation

The objective of a negotiation is for two or more parties to try to reach an agreement for mutual benefit. A common business phrase used stated that the outcome of a successful negotiation was a "win-win situation." In other words, each party benefited. This would seem to indicate that both parties have some areas where they may be more flexible, while others are mostly nonnegotiable, depending on whether it is a buyer's or seller's market.

The seller or supplier (hotel, facility, vendor for outside or off premise services) and the buyer (group planner) have different "hot buttons." Knowing whether it is a buyer's or seller's market will also put you at an advantage. Also, compare the proposals of three or more hotels to get a truer picture of the current market.

Attrition

Planner and facility negotiations center on each part of the final deal and contract content. Today, almost all contracts mention the terms attrition and attrition clause. These are the CLC definitions:

Attrition: The difference between the actual number of sleeping rooms picked up (or food-and-beverage covers or revenue projections) and the number or formulas agreed to in the terms of the facility's contract. Usually there is an allowable shortfall before damages are assessed.

Attrition Clause: Contract wording that outlines potential damages or fees that a party may be required to pay in the event that it does not fulfill minimum commitments in the contract.

In recent years, attrition has become the main topic of concern among both corporate and association meeting planners. Industry leaders say that there are two reasons why:

Many contracts were written during a strong economy when meeting attendance was high; large room locks were justified by past attendance history. However, the convention actually occurred during a "recession," when attendance is down.

The rates are likely also too high, compared not only to current hotel group rates but also the cheap rates often found on the same hotels' own Web site.

Figure 7.4 provides insight for both planners and hoteliers to facilitate contract development.

As these seven secrets show, the industry is constantly evolving and trying new strategies against which they gauge their attendees' responses. For associations especially, their success is measured in the actual convention attendance by their members.

Starting a Banquet Facility

Businesses rent banquet facilities for employee recognition ceremonies, team-building seminars and business meetings. Meanwhile, individuals and families rent banquet facilities for weddings, parties, and fundraisers. The fee for renting a banquet room can be as little as $100 to as much as $5000 a night, so renting out your own space can be lucrative. Consider starting your own banquet facility.

Instructions

Define your customer demographics. Make a list of the types of customers you want to attract. Call up other banquet facilities and speak with management to get an idea of the types of customers they do the most business with. Call up catering services and dig up information about the market conditions.

Find a location conducive to attracting the kind of customers you want. Look for large areas of open land if you want to offer outdoor dining. Also, look for old facilities you can buy and renovate.

Secure financing to buy the building, renovate the building or build a facility from the ground up. Apply for a bank loan at a traditional bank or an online lender.

Apply for licensing through the State Health Department and attend the required courses. Pay the health licensing fees. Fees vary from state to state and can range from $150 to $3000. In addition, fees may be due annually.

Work with a construction contractor to design a state-of-the-art facility, including the design of the kitchen, eating and entertainment areas. In the "Tinley Park Convention Center Market Study," researchers discovered banquet hall guests,"typically require a ballroom or multipurpose space where food and beverage services, and in some cases, entertainment can be provided."

Take your plans to the City or County Urban Planning and Development Department and apply for building and zoning permits.

Start construction and complete the building or renovations. Once complete, buy industrial kitchen equipment, such as exhaust fans, industrial refrigeration units and stoves. Be sure to review state standards for health and safety when ordering.

Install kitchen equipment. Then, schedule a health inspection with a state department representative. Make required adjustments if you don't pass the health inspection the first time.

Buy tables and chairs. In the book, "Hotel Convention Sales, Services, and Operations," Pat Golden-Romero writes that banquet round tables generally seat eight to 10 people. She also suggests menus should be decided in advance because it results "in better portion cost control."

Hire catering staff and servers. Advertise job openings in hospitality magazines or in the hospitality section of the employment classifieds of your city newspapers.

Market the facilities to event planners, wedding planners and business conference planners. Plan a tour of the newly-finished banquet facility. Print invitations with the banquet facilities name on them, then send them to reputable event planners in the state.

Gaylord Opryland Resort and Convention Center

Gaylord Opryland Resort & Convention Center, formerly known as Opryland Hotel, is a large hotel and convention center located in Nashville, Tennessee and owned by Gaylord Hotels, a division of Gaylord Entertainment Company. It is the largest non-casino hotel in the Continental United States outside of Las Vegas. The property, given a general theme toward "Southern hospitality", opened as The Opryland Hotel in 1977 adjacent to the Opryland USA theme park and the Grand Ole Opry house, from which the hotel took its name. The hotel originally featured 600 guest rooms, a 20,000-square-foot (1,900 m^2) ballroom, and 30,000 square feet (2,800 m^2) of convention space. Originally built by the National Life & Accident Insurance Company, Opryland Hotel was sold to then-Oklahoma City-based Gaylord Broadcasting Company (which soon after changed its name to Gaylord Entertainment Company) in 1982, along with most of National Life's entertainment properties, including WSM radio, Opryland USA, and the Grand Ole Opry.

In 1983, six years after opening, Opryland Hotel completed its first major expansion, dubbed "Phase II". This large undertaking added 467 guest rooms, moving the total to 1,067. Phase II also brought 30,000 square feet (2,800 m^2) more of ballroom space, and added the hotel's first signature atrium, the Garden Conservatory. Under large panes of glass and filled with plant life and fountains, the Garden Conservatory is designed to allow guests to experience a walk in a tropical garden without going outdoors. Hundreds of rooms have balconies overlooking the Conservatory. This was the first truly unique thing the hotel had to offer, and it set the stage for the next two expansions.

By 1988, Opryland Hotel had expanded to 1,891 guest rooms. In the "Phase III" expansion, another 18,000-square-foot (1,700 m^2) ballroom was added along with the Cascades, a second atrium designed to complement the Garden Conservatory. The Cascades is covered by an acre of glass, and features thousands of plant species and large artificial waterfalls. As part of Phase III, but delayed by one year, another 4,000-square-foot (370 m^2) ballroom opened, designed for more intimate settings and smaller functions.

Separate from the Phase III expansion was the addition of an 18 hole golf course, "Springhouse Golf Club", located 2 miles (3.2 km) east of the hotel. The par-72 links-style course was home to the BellSouth Senior Classic at Opryland on the Champions Tour from 1994 to 2003. It was renamed "Springhouse Links" in 2001, and then "Gaylord Springs" in 2006.

Opryland Hotel completed its "Phase IV" expansion in 1996. The $175-million "Delta" added 922 guest rooms, bringing the total to its current 2,881, and was the largest construction project in the history of Nashville at the time (it was eclipsed in 1999 by Adelphia Coliseum, now known as LP Field). Also part of the expansion, which more than doubled the size of the existing structure, was an additional 55,465-square-foot (5,152.9 m^2) ballroom, a 289,000-square-foot (26,800 m^2) exhibit hall, and the Delta Atrium. The 150-foot (46 m) tall, 4.5 acres (1.8 ha) atrium was given a Cajun theme, borrowing many elements from New Orleans,

Louisiana. Also under the large glass roof is the Delta River, a 0.25 miles (0.40 km) artificial waterway. For a $9 fee, guests may ride in a "Delta Flatboat" through a guided tour of the atrium. When it was christened, water samples from more than 1,700 rivers throughout the world, including every registered river in the United States, were poured into the Delta River.

The Delta expansion solidified the trend that Gaylord was focusing more efforts on its hotel division than its theme park, as the massive undertaking swallowed up any and all land the theme park could have expanded upon. Indeed, following the 1997 season, the Opryland USA theme park ceased operations and was demolished. Simultaneously, Gaylord Entertainment announced a joint venture with the Mills Corporation for construction of the 12,000,000-square-foot (1,100,000 m^2) Opry Mills shopping mall on the site. The park closure hurt occupancy rates at Opryland Hotel for the next five years. Gaylord Entertainment later divested its share of the mall and now leases the property and the "Opry" name to Simon Properties, the successor to Mills Corporation.

After the theme park closed, Gaylord considered taking the "Opryland" name off the hotel, since "Opryland" (a name which was considered to be most synonymous with the theme park) no longer existed. Extensive market research showed that the hotel would have to rebuild its reputation without the "Opryland" name, so it was kept.

In the late 1990s, Gaylord Entertainment acquired the Ramada Inn on McGavock Pike, just across the street from Opryland Hotel. It was given a major renovation and dropped its Ramada affiliation to be known simply as "The Inn at Opryland". It is now affiliated with Radisson Hotels. This motel is marketed toward guests wishing to receive Opryland Hotel quality and amenities at economy prices.

In 1999, the new Gaylord subsidiary "Opryland Lodging Group", which was formed in 1997 to plan expansions, was renamed "Opryland Hotels" as it began to see its plans for sister properties in Kissimmee, Florida and Grapevine, Texas come to fruition. Another hotel was later announced for Prince George's County, Maryland. As a result of these new plans, the hotel was renamed Opryland Hotel Nashville and given designation as the company's flagship property. The other hotels in the chain were to be named "Opryland Hotel Florida", "Opryland Hotel Texas" and "Opryland Hotel Potomac", respectively.

On October 26, 2001, Opryland Hotel Nashville was rebranded as Gaylord Opryland Resort & Convention Center (or Gaylord Opryland, for short), taking its name from its corporate parent. Gaylord Entertainment made the change seeking to take the "Opryland" name off of the new property in Florida. The Opryland Hotels division was renamed "Gaylord Hotels", and the Florida property was given the name "Gaylord Palms." The Texas hotel was initially going to be called "Gaylord Opryland Texas", but was later changed to "Gaylord Texan", after more market research concluded it needed an identity of its own. The yet-to-be-opened Maryland property was renamed "Gaylord National." Company officials at the time stated that the "Opryland" branding was strong to Nashville (and Texas, initially), but didn't fit with projects in other parts of the United States. Despite the rebranding effort, most locals (including the broadcast media) still refer to Gaylord Opryland as "Opryland Hotel."

In lieu of another expansion and as a result of the rebranding, the hotel underwent a $5 million renovation in 2003. With it came a refurbishment and rebranding of several of the hotel's restaurants and pubs, new retail establishments, and building improvements. Plans were also announced to renovate and refurnish all of the hotel's 2,881 guest rooms over the next few years.

According to a 2003 press release, Gaylord Opryland planned to build a 5,000-seat amphitheatre on the site in the near future, but those plans seem to have been abandoned in favor of a convention center expansion.

May 2010 Flood

On May 3, 2010 the entire Opryland Hotel complex and its surrounding campus—including Music Valley Drive and parts of Briley Parkway—was under 5-10 feet of floodwaters generated from the swollen Cumberland River, which jumped its banks after two days of torrential rainfall. Pictures from the inside of the hotel showed the Cascades restaurant area swamped with water and debris, as were the adjacent tropical gardens. Aerial shots confirm the entire complex, as well as the nearby Opry Mills Mall, was completely inundated by water. Gaylord's other riverfront properties—Springhouse Golf Course, and The Wildhorse Saloon—are also directly affected by the flooding Cumberland River. The golf course was completely underwater, and Wildhorse Saloon was partially flooded along First Avenue in downtown Nashville. (WKRN, WSMV, WTVF) The Gaylord Opryland Hotel reopened its doors on November 15, 2010.

Future Expansion

On February 12, 2007, Gaylord Hotels announced plans to expand Gaylord Opryland once again, this time focusing on the Convention Center. The $400 million expansion would have nearly doubled the size of the existing Convention Center and added a 400-room, stand-alone, all-suite hotel. A large parking garage would also have been added to the site. The expansion will be built on the south side of the existing structure, pushing the building more toward Opry Mills. The plans hinged on $80 million in public financing through the Metro government that would be repaid through the property taxes generated by the expansion. The first step in this process would be getting the Tennessee General Assembly to designate the site a "special tourism development zone".

This expansion would have also made Gaylord Opryland the largest convention hotel outside of Las Vegas. It was expected to be completed by 2010,but following the economic slowdown of 2008-2009 and the May 2010 flood, the plans are on indefinite hold.

Hotel Areas

Unlike its sister properties, Gaylord Opryland has no universal structure layout as a result of its continued expansion. Because of this, the property can be very confusing to navigate, even for frequent visitors. Employees are even said to get lost in the hotel from time to time.

1. **Magnolia** - The original lobby and retail area of the hotel. Currently features "The District" and Grand Staircase, modeled after the Tara from Gone With the Wind.
2. **Garden Conservatory** - The first atrium constructed, considered by many to be the heart of the hotel. Several weddings take place in the Garden Conservatory's romantic setting each year, near the Lionhead Fountain and Crystal Gazebo.
3. **Cascades** - The second atrium constructed. Features the rotating Cascades Terrace Lounge as well as Wasabe (a Japanese sushi restaurant) and the hotel's largest waterfalls. Connects to the main lobby, which is where the main, and only, registration desk is located.
4. **Delta** - The third and largest atrium constructed. Currently the center of activity at Gaylord Opryland. Home to the Delta River, several retail stores, a few

eateries, and Gaylord Opryland's finest restaurant, the Old Hickory Steakhouse. This area of the hotel also features a connection to Opry Mills Shopping Mall. The Delta project was the main inspiration for the company's expansion into other markets.

4. **Convention Center** - The largest convention area in Tennessee with three main exhibit areas and five ballrooms.

Convention Center

The Convention Center at Gaylord Opryland is in direct competition with the Metro government-owned Nashville Convention Center. Gaylord Opryland is built to handle large conventions, while the NCC is suited more for smaller gatherings. Nashville is currently considering plans to expand or replace the existing public convention center, claiming they are unable to attract major conventions due to the center's relatively small size. In contrast, Gaylord Opryland has expanded its convention center twice since NCC opened in downtown Nashville in 1987 and regularly attracts major conventions to the city.

Gaylord Opryland currently features three exhibit halls and five ballrooms. Coupled with its massive hotel, Gaylord Opryland Convention Center can easily accommodate upwards of 10-12 separate gatherings at one time. On most weekends, guests will find at least two conventions taking place.

The convention center is divided into five areas: the Magnolia, Tennessee, Presidents, Governors, and Delta sections; each of which specializes in terms of rooms' size, and purposes. There are currently three levels in the convention center to accommodate the variation in height among the different ballrooms and exhibit halls.

The hotel currently boasts 109,465 square feet (10,169.6 m^2) of ballroom space and 319,000 square feet

(29,600 m^2) of exhibit space. A planned expansion will nearly double its size.

Local Purposes

While Gaylord Opryland caters largely to the out-of-town convention market, it serves a large purpose for the local community as well. Many local high schools use the ballroom space for their yearly proms. It is also known for being one of Nashville's hottest "first-date" spots because of its central location, restaurants, walkways, and scenery. Many local companies also take advantage of the Convention Center's abundant meeting space. Unlike most other non-casino hotels, a sizable portion of Gaylord Opryland's visitors are not actually guests of the hotel. The scenery of the various atria along with the various shops and dining options attract many walk-in visitors to the hotel every day. Outside vendor Town Parke currently charges $18 to park automobiles at the hotel , but locals have found a way around this charge by parking at nearby Opry Mills free of charge and walking the short path to Gaylord Opryland. This is not recommended for overnight stays, both for lack of security, and the risk of being towed. Valet parking service is also available to hotel guests for $25 a night.

A Country Christmas

During the months of November, December, and through mid-January of each year, Gaylord Opryland attracts thousands of visitors to see the large display of Christmas decorations, dubbed *A Country Christmas*. Millions of decorative lights are placed in the trees at the resort, and all three atria contain various decorations, including animatronics. The hotel begins installing lights in July of each year. In addition, several special holiday-themed shows and attractions take place, including ICE!, a display of ice sculptures, and the Radio City Rockettes Christmas Spectacular. During the Christmas seasons of 2007 and 2008, ICE! has had a theme of Dr. Suess's How the Grinch Stole Christmas, The season of 2009 had a theme of A Charlie Brown Christmas, and 2010 had a theme of Santa Claus is Comin' to Town. 2010 marked the 27th anniversary of Gaylord Opryland's *A Country Christmas*.

Features

1. Home to the studios of 650 WSM, the company-owned 50 kW clear channel country music radio station.
2. Light and dancing water shows can be found in the Delta and Cascades atria.
3. 238 pieces of art from 207 artists, all from Tennessee.
4. 0.25-mile (0.40 km) "river", home to several fish species.
5. Adjacent to Grand Ole Opry and Opry Mills.
6. Adjacent to Cumberland River, though it is not visible from within the hotel.
7. Summerfest, a little block party, featuring real dancers and performers, happens every Summer in the Delta atrium, near the Haggen-Dazs & Opry Shop.

Specifications

1. 2,881 guest rooms, including:
   (a) 200+ suites
   (b) 750+ atrium-facing rooms with private balconies, patios, or large bay windows which overhang into the atrium
2. 109,465 square feet (10,170 m^2) of ballroom space

3. 319,000 square feet (30,000 m²) of exhibit space
4. 6 full-service restaurants which include Ristorante Volare, The Old Hickory Steakhouse, Cascades American Cafe, Rusty's Sports Bar, Water's Edge Marketplace Buffet, and Findley's Irish Pub.
5. 3 lounges which The Cascades Terrace Lounge, The Jack Daniel's Saloon, and The Library at Old Hickory
6. 8 eateries which include STAX Hamburgers, Paisano's Pizza, Häagen-Dazs, Christie Cookies, Conservatory Café, Wasabi's Sushi, Java Coast Coffee, and Godiva Chocolatier.
7. 14 retail stores including Amelia's, Savannah's and Miss Scarlet's, the three of which are women's fashions stores, Alexzander Kalifano's, a jewelry shop, the Cascades, Magnolia, and Delta Necessities Stores, Cowboys and Angels, Delta Gifts and Decor, Bushels and Baskets, The Opry Shop, Bookmark, Sunny G Children's Boutique, Gaylord Springs Golf Shop and coming in April 2010 Johnston & Murphy.
8. Fuse Nashville Nightclub which specializes in an assortment of gourmet food and cocktails, including the signature "Cotton Candy Martini".
9. Relâche Spa and Salon which offers a variety of massages and upscale services featuring a full-service salon, sauna, shopping boutique, as well as a fitness center which is open 24 hours. Relâche also houses the hotel's indoor pool and one of the outdoor pools.
10. The Arcade which features many games and prizes.

7

Role of Convention Sales Manager

A Manager is the person responsible for planning and directing the work of a group of individuals, monitoring their work, and taking corrective action when necessary. For many people, this is their first step into a management career. Managers may direct workers directly or they may direct several supervisors who direct the workers. The manager must be familiar with the work of all the groups he/she supervises, but does not need to be the best in any or all of the areas. It is more important for the manager to know how to manage the workers than to know how to do their work well.

A manager may have the power to hire or fire employees or to promote them. In larger companies, a manager may only recommends such action to the next level of management. The manager has the authority to change the work assignments of team members. A manager's title reflects what he/she is responsible for. An Accounting Manager supervises the Accounting function. An Operations Manager is responsible for the operations of the company. The Manager of Design Engineering supervises engineers and support staff engaged in design of a product or service. A Night Manager is responsible for the activities that take place at night. There are many management functions in business and, therefore, many manager titles. Regardless of title, the manager is responsible for planning, directing, monitoring and controlling the people and their work.

Basic Management Skill: Plan

Management starts with planning. Good management starts with good planning. And proper prior planning prevents... well, you know the rest of that one.

Without a plan you will never succeed. If you happen to make it to the goal, it will have been by luck or chance and is not repeatable. You may make it as a flash-in-the-pan, an overnight sensation, but you will never have the track record of accomplishments of which success is made.

Figure out what your goal is (or listen when your boss tells you). Then figure out the best way to get there. What resources do you have? What can you get? Compare strengths and weaknesses of individuals and other resources. Will putting four workers on a task that takes 14 hours cost less than renting a machine that can do the same task with one worker in 6 hours? If you change the first shift from an 8 AM start to a 10 AM start, can they handle the early evening rush so you don't have to hire an extra person for the second shift?

Look at all the probable scenarios. Plan for them. Figure out the worst possible scenario and plan for that too. Evaluate your different plans and develop what, in your best judgement, will work the best and what you will do if it doesn't.

Basic Management Skill: Organize

Now that you have a plan, you have to make it happen. Is everything ready ahead of your group so the right stuff will get to your group at the right time? Is your group prepared to do its part of the plan? Is the downstream organization ready for what your group will deliver and when it will arrive?

Are the workers trained? Are they motivated? Do they have the equipment they need? Are there spare parts available for the equipment? Has purchasing ordered the material? Is it the right stuff? Will it get here on the appropriate schedule?

Do the legwork to make sure everything needed to execute the plan is ready to go, or will be when it is needed. Check back to make sure that everyone understands their role and the importance of their role to the overall success.

Basic Management Skill: Direct

Now flip the "ON" switch. Tell people what they need to do. I like to think of this part like conducting an orchestra. Everyone in the orchestra has the music in front of them. They know which section is playing which piece and when. They know when to come in, what to play, and when to stop again. The conductor cues each section to make the music happen. That's your job here. You've given all your musicians (workers) the sheet music (the plan). You have the right number of musicians (workers) in each section (department), and you've arranged the sections on stage so the music will sound best (you have organized the work). Now you need only to tap the podium lightly with your baton to get their attention and give the downbeat.

Basic Management Skill: Monitor

Now that you have everything moving, you have to keep an eye on things. Make sure everything is going according to the plan. When it isn't going according to plan, you need to step in and adjust the plan, just as the orchestra conductor will adjust the tempo.

Problems will come up. Someone will get sick. A part won't be delivered on time. A key customer will go bankrupt. That is why you developed a contingency plan in the first place. You, as the manager, have to be always aware of what's going on so you can make the adjustments required.

This is an iterative process. When something is out of sync, you need to Plan a fix, Organize the resources to make it work, Direct the people who will make it happen, and continue to Monitor the effect of the change.

What do I want to do?

Perhaps the first thing you need to do is to figure out what you want your people to accomplish. A mission statement is a short document that tells your people, your customers (internal and external), and your suppliers what you are about. It makes it easier for everyone to pull together if everyone knows what the objective is. How to Draft a Mission Statement lists twelve things you can do to start drafting a mission statement for your group.

How Should I Set it up?

After you figure out where you are going and you write up your mission statement, you need to look at whether your organization supports that objective. If your organization does not support your objective, you need to change it so it does. When you have rearranged your organization so it does support your objective, you need to communicate that organization structure to everyone involved. This is done through an organization chart, an org chart for short. How to Build an Org Chart is a quick guideline on how to draw an org chart for a department. You can easily expand it out for an entire company.

How Does this look?

If anyone in your organization deals with the public, you should have a dress code for all employees. A dress code is a simple document that tells people in various functions what is appropriate work attire, and why. How to Set a Dress Code guides you through the steps of creating a workable dress code for your company.

Supervisor

A supervisor is the lowest, or most-junior, management position. It is usually a step above lead (Accounting Supervisor is senior to Lead Accounting Specialist), but below Manager.

A supervisor is responsible for the day-to-day performance of a small group. It may be a team, or a shift. The supervisor has experience in what the group does, but is not necessarily better at it than everyone he/she supervises. The supervisor's job is to guide the group toward its goals, see that all members of the team are productive, and resolve problems as they arise.

A supervisor generally does not have the power to hire or fire employees or to promote them. A supervisor usually recommends such action to the next level of management. The supervisor does, however, often have the authority to change the work roles of the members of the team, for instance deciding which individual will work at which station.

Senior Manager

Senior Manager is a title given in a large company with a perceived need for additional levels in its management structure. In a hierarchy, Senior Manager falls between Manager and General Manger. The Senior Manager, like all managers, is responsible for planning and directing the work of a group of individuals, monitoring their work, and taking corrective action when necessary.

Senior Managers may direct workers directly or they may direct several supervisors who direct the workers. The Senior Manager often supervises the largest or most important group in a company.

A Senior Manager may usually has the power to hire or fire employees or to promote them. The Senior Manager has the authority to change the work assignments of team members.

A Senior Manager's title reflects what he/she is responsible for. A Senior Accounting Manager supervises a major accounting function. The Senior Manager of Design Engineering may supervise engineers and support staff engaged in design of a company's flagship product or service. Regardless of title, a Senior Manager is responsible for planning, directing, monitoring and controlling the people and their work.

General Manager

A General Manager has broad, overall responsibility for a business or organization. Whereas a manager may be responsible for one functional area, the General Manager is responsible for all areas.

General Managers manage through subordinate manager. However, a General Manager may have individuals reporting to him/her who are not managers. A General Manager has the power to hire, fire, or promote employees. A General Manager is responsible for higher level planning than a manager. A General Manager is often responsible for the overall strategic planning and direction of the company or organization and leaves the day-to-day management of the various functions to the managers.

The Role Of Convention Bureaus

Over the years convention and visitors bureaus (CVBs), also known as housing bureaus, have evolved to service their markets more effectively. Originally, bureaus were created in large U.S. cities to promote their destination to convention groups needing hotel guest rooms and meeting facilities. As the name implies, the term visitors refers more to the tourism promotion. Convention bureaus can be funded through different sources. Some are organizations to which local hotels, attractions, convention facilities, and services become members and pay fees. Some are funded through local room tax proceeds, which are paid by tourists (or anyone else) staying in the hotels. Yet, another funding source can be from publicly funded and built exhibition halls. In the 1980s and 1990s, many smaller cities were able to get convention centers built primarily through this method.

Regardless of the funding sources, the main mission of the convention bureau is to promote and market that destination and its visitor services. The visitors can be convention delegates, tourists, or both. If, after the meeting, some attendees stay a day or two and visit local tourist attractions, the CVB has accomplished one of its objectives.

Figure 5.1 is an example of an organizational chart from a membership structured bureau. In this type of organization the members are on top. This model illustrates the decision and policy-making structure for the board of directors and CEO. There are usually two or three different operational departments. A bureau's primary program is that of marketing a destination as a meeting and vacation venue. The sales and marketing department is primarily responsible for identifying, developing, and obtaining commitments and then providing servicing and support.

The marketing and communications department has a multitude of responsibilities directly related to the development of bureau publications and the writing of news stories and press releases. Other key areas include telling the bureau's story not only to its own community, but also to the trade and consumer markets.

Site Inspections and Familiarization Tours

In recent years, site inspections have become an industry standard. Conducted by the meeting planner, it is an in-depth tour and evaluation of a hotel under consideration for an event. Examples of site inspection standard guidelines and recommended facilities and services to be evaluated are included in the addendum. The site inspection typically occurs after there has been a confirmation that accommodations and event space are available for the dates sought by the group. The hotel sales manager, along with the convention services coordinator, will conduct the inspection. If the CVB was the first point of contact for the meeting planner, it will usually coordinate the inspections at each hotel. A CVB should always be involved in planning the inspection itinerary when it is anticipated that multiple hotels will be utilized for citywide conventions. With this type of planner the CVB representative will most probably pick up the planner at the airport and escort him or her for the entire tour.

On the other hand, a familiarization (or "fam") tour is often the first introduction to the destination, whether hotels or tourism attractions or both. Originally a tool used by destination marketing organizations to familiarize travel agents, now group meeting/event planners are being offered fams.

Figure 5.3 is an example of a promotion advertisement, in the form of an invitation. The invitation was placed in a monthly trade publication that many professional meeting planners read. The fam is for all types of meeting and event planners to attend in Jamaica. Events such as this often are jointly sponsored by the publication, destination marketing organization, and area hotels and meeting facilities.

Destination Marketing Organizations

The other category of destination marketing organization (DMO) is a tourism or travel office. Their promotional focus is primarily on developing the leisure visitor, but we will briefly discuss these organizations here, as they work closely with a CVB. Many of these tourism organizations throughout the world operate independently from each other. Scope and jurisdiction vary widely. he one common thread is that each receives some level of governmental funding. As many travel tourism professionals know, many regions of the United States (and other countries) have a hotel room or so-called "tourist tax" law in place. This funding source is rapidly diminishing or being redirected as local governments seek viable alternatives to their own state budget cuts.

The current situation at many destinations is that there may no longer be both a CVB and a separate tourism or DMO office. Therefore, both meeting planners and hotel sales and convention services professionals must research which local tourism organization can provide the materials and resources they need to ensure the success of each event.

Industry Insider

How buyers and sellers "find each other" . . . it's no secret that meeting planners get frustrated with hotel sales managers who don't do their homework. Qualifying the lead before you contact them means you have hotel rooms and event facilities large enough to accommodate their needs. On the other hand, a lead from a CVB is prequalified and a streamlined way for the buyer and seller to find each other.

Leads Programs

In some cities the convention and visitors bureau will offer a leads program. Leads generated by their own convention sales department will be sent to member hotels and related services, that pay to receive them. Any of the recipient hotels that subsequently book rooms from this lead in turn will pay a fee or percentage to the convention bureau on the total rooms utilized.

Destination Management Company (DMC)

A professional services company possessing extensive local knowledge, expertise, and resources, specializing in the design and implementation of events, activities, tours, transportation, and program logistics. Depending on the company and the staff specialists in the company, they offer, but are not limited to, the following: creative proposals for special events within the meeting; guest tours; VIP amenities and transportation; shuttle services; staffing within convention centers and hotels; teambuilding, golf outings and other activities; entertainment, including sound and lighting; décor and theme development; ancillary meetings and management professionals; and advance meetings and onsite registration services and housing.

8

Convention Sales in Hotels

Prepare the Guest Room

A little planning goes a long way. Reduce stress for both you and your guests by preparing ahead of time for their arrival. Even when it is obvious that you've taken measures to plan, guests can still feel like outsiders in your home. If they have to search for clean towels, sneak downstairs for water in the middle of the night or hunt for a bar of soap, they will feel awkward doing it. The most hospitable thing you can do as host or hostess is to properly organize a room that makes them feel welcome:

1. Make sure the bed in your guest room is comfortable. If it's not, consider purchasing a two inch memory foam mattress pad to place on top.
2. Use your best quality, freshly laundered sheets for visitors and provide them with a variety of pillows. Down alternative works well in case of allergies, and at least two per guest please. Clean blankets are a must and let your visitors know where there are extras just in case.
3. Find an obvious place to put a nice set of matching towels. Your guests won't be able to locate them if you've left them on the top shelf of the closet.

1. Place books or current magazines in a basket or decorative box along with several bottles of water and some individual size snacks in case of a midnight hunger attack.
2. Important extras include: an alarm clock, a box of tissues, and if you really want to impress; most chocolate stores will have cute little boxes that you can fill to casually set on the night table.

Don't Leave Things Until the Last Minute

Nothing says, "We've been *so* looking forward to your visit," like having your guests stand in the hallway while you apologetically change the sheets on the bed they are about to sleep on. Additionally, if the guest room is ready ahead of time and something unexpected arises, you will have one less thing to worry about.

Food Allergies

Before stocking the refrigerator and planning meals, find out if your guests have any food requirements, allergies, or dislikes. If your guests are early risers, they won't want you setting the alarm to get up at the crack of dawn; but do show them where they can find coffee, cereal, juice and anything else they might want for breakfast. In most cases, they will be happy to look after themselves and may even have the coffee waiting for you when you get up. With a little extra effort and planning, your visitors will feel completely at home thanks to your considerate hospitality.

Instructions

Get ready ahead of time so your guests feel welcome instead of in the way. Clean the house and clear the clutter from your guest room. Fresh flowers, candles and chocolates are all thoughtful, welcoming touches.

Make an extra set of house keys for your guests so they can come and go as they please. Not only is this a generous gesture, but it will free you up.

Buy an inflatable air mattress to supplement sleepovers. They're inexpensive, comfortable and can be re-inflated at the touch of a button. Well before guests arrive, inflate the mattress outside and let the smell leach out. Lie down and check for leaks.

Place a basket of sample-size shampoos, soaps and lotions near a stack of fresh towels for guests' convenience.

Set up a small television (with headphones) in the guest room in the event that your guests have trouble sleeping or wake much earlier than the rest of the household. Include some books and magazines.

Draw up a map of your neighborhood and environs, pointing out points of interest. Purchase a guidebook and flag any special places or activities your guests would be interested in.

Provide a surface or suitcase rack where guests can open their luggage so they don't have to spread out their belongings all over the floor. Clear out part of the closet and provide hangers.

Give guests the grand tour. Point out where glasses, dishes and silverware are kept, as well as tea, coffee, cereal and doughnuts. Encourage early risers to help themselves.

Put the coffeemaker on a timer to start up in the morning, or get it ready to go with a flip of the switch.

Let guests know what to expect as far as household schedules are concerned. Clarify when people get up and go to bed, and mention any special events that are in the works to minimize miscommunications. See 68 Set Up a Bathroom Schedule.

Challenges

1. Make Room: You've turned the guest-room closet and dresser into backup storage for your stuff — but there's an easy way to give visitors a place to hang clothes and stash socks. Take 10 or so full hangers from the middle of the closet, and rubber-band them together in a couple of smaller bunches; then temporarily relocate them to your own room or even the basement. Tuck several empty hangers into the newly opened space. Also, empty the contents of the top dresser drawer into a box, and slip it under the bed or onto the closet floor. (If this room has collected everything from your son's outgrown ice hockey skates to that fabric you plan to use someday, box it up and take it out.) Finish by setting a pretty dish on the bureau to hold guests' jewelry and loose change.

2. Dress the Bed: Kudos to you if you planned ahead and put on clean sheets after the last visitors left (and if not, now's the time). Even so, the bedding could probably use some sprucing. Pop the pillows (any type but foam) with cases on into the dryer on the low-heat setting for about five minutes to de-dust and fluff them — the shape of the pillows will actually help pull wrinkles out of the cases as they tumble. Replace the winter comforter with a lighter blanket. As you make up the bed, spritz some linen spray or Febreze Fabric Refresher ($5 for a 27-ounce bottle), which gets rid of odors instead of just masking them, on the fitted sheet. If your guest quarters are a sofa bed, open it up and run a hand vacuum over any crevices where dust, crumbs, and stray coins may have collected.

3. Spiff up surfaces. First, turn on all the lights and pull up the blinds so you can see where the dust has settled — before guests do. Use a microfiber cloth to whisk furniture tops, lamp bases, the headboard, and any framed pictures or mirrors. Eyeball the ceiling for dangling cobwebs and zap them with the cloth on the end of a broom. If the blinds are dusty, flip them the other way. Empty the wastebasket; put in a clean liner. Finally, vacuum, but only in the middle of the room, where dirt is most noticeable. Back up to the door as you work, so you can step out at the end without leaving footprints on the carpet.

Hotel Meeting Room and Convention Planning

The convention sales department must work closely with the director of sales to ensure that the blocking and control of function space doesn't lose sight of the goal: maximizing revenue. In this article we will discuss the considerations to be made to effectively assign space. This article in particular has an extensive glossary from the Convention Industry Council (CIC)–APEX approved definitions list. Finally, we will discuss these terms and where they fit into the convention services meeting setup process.

The First Step

The first contact between the convention services department and meeting planner will be between a few weeks or a few months after the event has been confirmed. This length of time will be determined by

1. The size of the group and the function space needed
2. The actual event date

For larger conventions, booked years in advance, contact will be minimal until approximately one year before the event. As the event approaches, the meeting planner will contact a hotel group coordinator about their guest room block needs. These areas are discussed in other articles, but note that many properties have combined these functions to minimize frustration for the planner. Therefore, the hotel event contact assigned to this group must be completely knowledgeable, regardless of his or her title.

Types of Function Rooms

The function setup terminology has changed over the years as many more design options in furniture, lighting, and AV become standard. However, some of the most common styles and their names have not. The complete definitions from the CIC Glossary are listed at the end of this article.

Setup Styles

In the next sections, following each style description is the corresponding diagram with the common variations using standard hotel and convention industry terminology. These diagrams are not to scale and should be used only as a guideline. Keep in mind that room capacity and aisle sizes are regulated by local fire departments. This information is usually also listed on the Meeting room capacity guide provided in a group convention sales kit.

Figures 9.1 and 9.2 are examples of the room specifications and capacity sheets for a 100-room hotel with a 1,830 square foot (approximately) conference center.

The diagram in the bottom of Figure 9.1 shows the common table and chair setup styles.

The diagram in Figure 9.2 shows the actual dimensions of the meeting and function space, along with the room capacity chart on a two-sided brochure card.

Meeting Room Set-ups and Styles

Auditorium Style

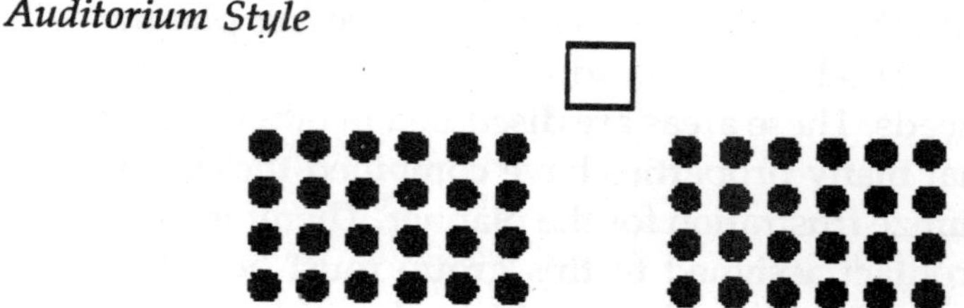

Appropriate for short lecture or larger groups that do not require extensive note-taking.

Banquet Style

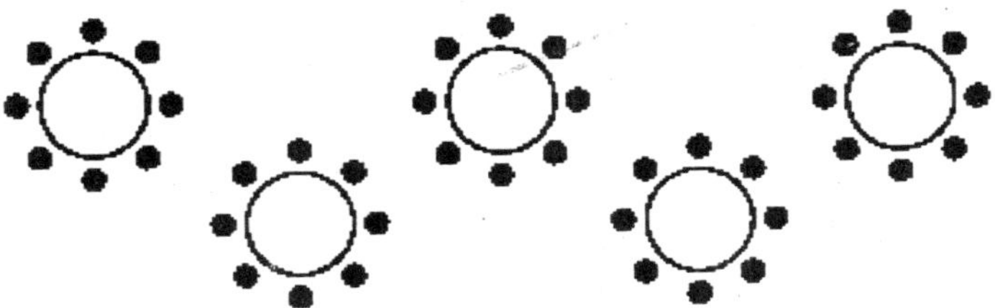

Used for meals and small groups discussions. 5' rounds seat eight people comfortably.

Hollow Square Style

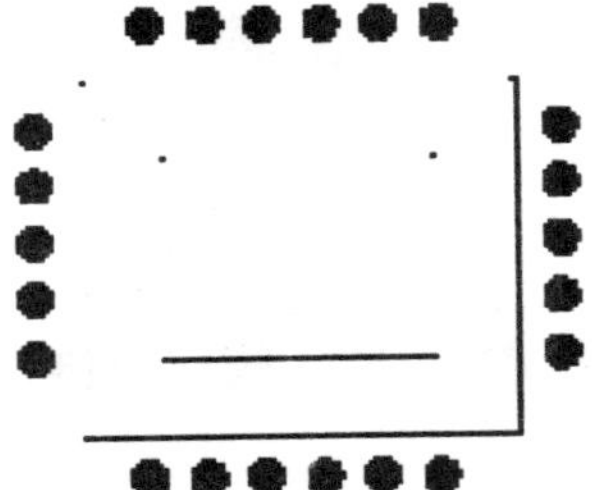

Appropriate for groups fewer than 40 where there is a group leader or panel seated at the head of the set up.

Classroom

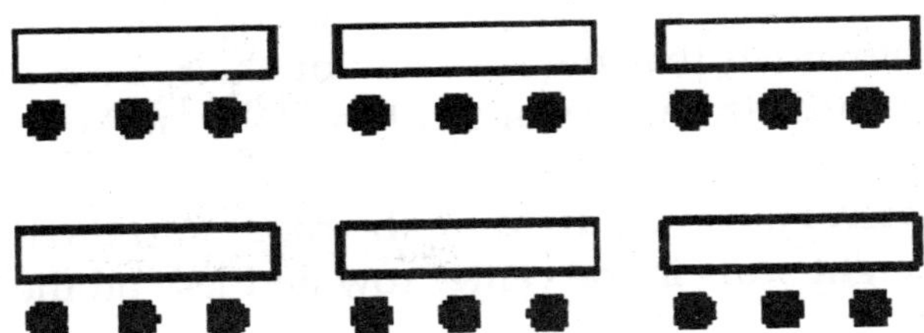

Most desirable for long lectures. For large numbers tables will need to be rented.

U-Shape Style

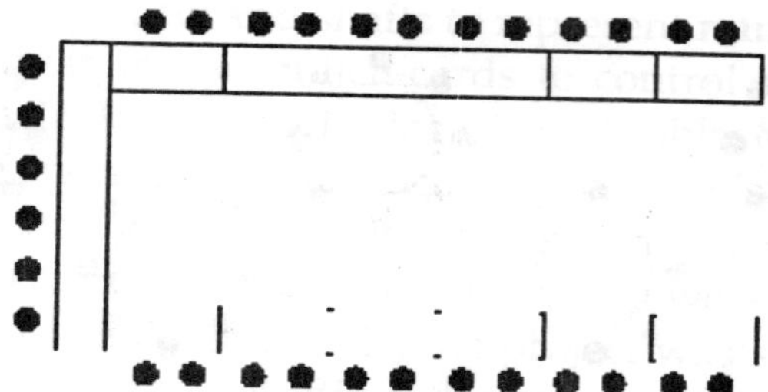

Conference Style

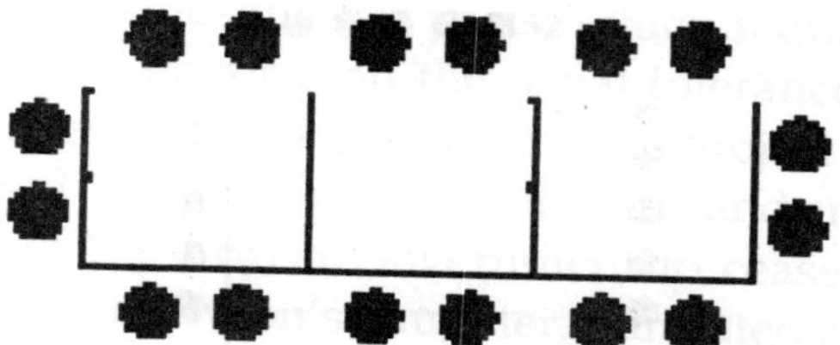

Theater or Auditorium Style

These names are used interchangeably. This style requires only chairs, which are set up in rows. The chairs face the speaker or stage, typically in the front of the room. Theater style is used for general sessions for small or large groups, which require limited or no note-taking. It is recommended that the first row of chairs be no less than six feet back from the stage or head table at the front of the room. The most popular setup uses a center aisle, like in a theater. However, dividing the room into three sections, with eight seats in the center row and less on the outsides is popular as well. Variations on this style include senate, semicircular, and v-shaped. Each is used to increase the viewing area for attendees. As with each setup presented here, the CSM will know each room in the facility best. Inexperienced meeting planners therefore should rely on their expertise.

One big drawback of theater style is the difficulty for attendees in the rear rows to see the front stage area. If possible, the stage or head table area (used for seated speakers or a panel) should be put on risers to increase their visibility.

A multimedia presentation format, using large screens and power point, is recommended for large groups in most styles of setup. The distinguishing factor from theater style is the addition of tables. These are usually used for longer meetings or training sessions that require extensive writing or note-taking.

Setup Styles with Tables

Schoolroom or classroom: These names are used interchangeably. This style requires narrow tables, known as classroom tables, either six or eight feet in length, to be set up with chairs in rows that are facing the front of the room or stage. It is equally as common a style as the theater setup, but needed only for longer sessions that require note-taking. This setup is the standard for training meetings, but a big drawback is the amount of space needed. Additional table setups possible for this style include perpendicular or V-shaped.

Conference style: Also referred to as board of directors. This setup is so popular with smaller groups (10–20 people) that many forward-thinking hotels now have a permanent meeting room space outfitted with a rectangular "boardroom" table and comfortable seating. Hotels need function space to be flexible, so rectangular classroom or banquet tables are substituted when a permanent table isn't available.

U-shape or horseshoe: When a face-to-face design is needed for small groups, the U-shape is a common solution. It is also known as a horseshoe, because of its shape. If the group is large, an inside and outside U-shape may be recommended. In general the U-shape is well suited for board meetings with AV presentations.

Hollow square and hollow circular: This is similar to the U-shape, except the open end is closed. This style is a good choice when a head table area isn't necessary. This setup historically has been used with multiple monitors/ VCRs/DVDs/CDs set up inside the hollow for comfortable viewing from all seats.

Seat Distance

The distance between each seat for each style mentioned in this section varies. Planners can obtain the complete function room equipment list, which includes table sizes, dimensions, and types from the CSM. They will know best how to set up each room to achieve the goal of comfort desired for each attendee. The recommended guideline is 24 to 36 inches of space per attendee between chairs. Function room size, layout, and any restrictions that impact the line of sight must be considered.

Table Spacing and Placement

Spacing guidelines are also contained in the complete function room equipment list. Additionally, the function layout in their collateral material will include diagrams that show examples. Planners also should check on diagrams available through the sales or catering department software used by that property. The recommended guideline is nine feet from the center of one table to the next one. Keep in mind that the size of the table will vary, based on what the hotel uses; the two sizes most commonly used are described next.

Banquet Setup Styles

Food and beverage functions can require tables, or chairs, or both, depending on the type of event being held by the planner. As with meeting functions, the CSM will know the best setup design for the particular room being used for each function. Commonly used setups include the following:

Banquet round tables: These come in two sizes, with the smaller one comfortably seating eight and the larger up to 10 people. They are used for sit-down or buffet dinners. Note: Round tables are also commonly used for meetings that are known as Round Table meetings. After the meeting, these tables can remain in the room and be used for a food function. This is an efficient way to maximize room use for small groups who need to control their meeting room rental costs. Examples of a banquet round table layout are provided in Figure 9.5, as part of a floor plan.

Buffet tables: These are used most commonly for the buffet food lines or displays. A popular variation is a circular buffet table setup. This can be achieved by using banquet rounds or serpentine tables shaped like a big S.

Function Room Assignments

The CSM or event manager is in charge of function room assignments. The exact meeting room location (name) usually is not assigned until a few months prior to arrival or later, depending on the size of the group. Some of the criteria to be considered include:

1. Size and capacity under required room setup (fire code compliant)
2. Type of event/presentation style
3. Room location with regard to traffic
4. Room location with regard to who's next door
5. Move-in and move-out dates of other groups

It is important for the event or hotel CSM to be knowledgeable in audiovisual terminology and requirements. This is true regardless of whether the AV equipment is owned by the facility or an outside AV services company is used. Almost all meetings today require some AV equipment, so it is important to understand the different types available, the different sources that supply it, and what to charge for equipment. This section presents the central issues in this crucial aspect of meeting management.

Audiovisual Requirements and Equipment

When a new hotel is being built, management is faced with a large decision:

Either to purchase AV equipment and hire staff to manage and service that department, or to select an outside vendor AV company from whom they will order the equipment.

The final decision will vary, depending on the type of facility: conference center, resort destination, or convention hotel. Other issues to consider are the standard policies of that hotel or conference center chain and their philosophy and commitment to servicing groups. Other considerations are:

1. Cost of equipment. Will the use justify the purchase of many different items?
2. Is there adequate, secured storage in the hotel?

3. What will be the labor cost to staff an in-house AV department?
4. Is there a reliable local AV vendor to contract with?
5. What method are your competitors using?
6. What discounts or commissions are part of the AV contract or associated costs?

One convention services manager in Lake Tahoe, Nevada, had this to say about finally deciding to go in-house: "We are in a very isolated area, so each time I need to order a single piece of equipment due to a group change, the service charge is outrageous. The AV company's office is in Reno, 35 miles away, and the weather can be a factor on equipment delivery nine months out of the year."

In evaluating whether to use an outside AV company, isolated destination resorts also have to consider "minimum orders" set by firms to cover their own costs. All properties must forecast projections for tentative/definite group meetings and future AV equipment needs.

Changing Technology

Not so long ago, AV was meant to supplement and support the actual presentation. The capabilities of the latest AV multimedia equipment now have become the news themselves. Most attendees now either bring their laptops along during the meeting or demand a "cyber computer bank" so they can quickly check their e-mail during meeting breaks. With that in mind, the following will provide an overview of the standard AV equipment used by hotels for meeting. A list of useful Web sites is provided at the end of this article for additional information on the use of meeting technology. In addition to learning what is available, some sources provide a link to a Web site for a free CD demo disk so you can evaluate the technology and decide if it's right for you.

Teleconferencing

Teleconferencing first gained interest in the 1980s, but lost popularity when it was much too expensive for meeting use. As the price has been lowered through improved technology, so has its acceptance increased. The events of 9/11 and subsequent increased worldwide travel security and delays have made "virtual meetings" and the use of teleconferencing much more attractive. The objective to have a meeting available in different areas through the use of telephone linkages with computer and AV equipment is now pursued quite extensively. For example, the AV equipment in this case could be a mini camera or a mini webcam placed on the computer PC with the picture or image projected to other meeting attendees simultaneously around the world.

Teleconferencing has evolved into videoconferencing as that technology has become more feasible. Academic users are now the emerging leader in some of these applications. College students now regularly complete some of their required courses online without ever seeing the teacher. Video lectures, discussions, and chats done in live time enhance the learning experience. Here is a web page from a company that provides a wide variety of video and satellite conferencing services.

Insiders' Tip

Many colleges and universities worldwide book meeting groups during the summer break. Most have very reasonable meeting and meal packages with access to this technology in an educational retreat atmosphere. Better yet, a number of these school offer degrees in Hotel or Convention Management, so they know the importance of properly servicing meeting groups! Most schools with meeting facilities belong to a national organization.

To use the present teleconferencing or videoconferencing technology in your upcoming meeting, ask the CSM or event manager. He or she most likely has handled your type of equipment needs before. The equipment description and pricing schedule, whether in-house or through an outside AV contractor, will be your best resource. Figure 9.4 shows a hotel AV equipment list. In this example, Show Time Audio Visual Equipment provides the actual equipment to meeting groups at the hotel.

Types of Audiovisual Equipment Screens

Note: Check on the ceiling setup of the room to be used onsite. Review the banquet chart for sizing.

Wall or ceiling screens: Designed to be hung from hooks or lines mounted on the wall or ceiling.

Tripod screens: Mounted permanently on a tripod stand so they are portable; ideal for smaller meeting rooms.

Screen Fabrics

1. Silver metallic and lenticular surfaces offer maximum brilliance and wideangle consistency but are more expensive than other types.
2. Matte-surface screens offer consistent brilliance from a wider angle.
3. Glass-beaded screens offer greater brilliance.

Setup Guidelines

1. Five-feet principle: Bottom of the screen must be a minimum of five feet off the floor.
2. One-by-six principle: No one should be seated closer than one times the screen's width and no farther than six times the screen's width.

Types of Projection

Rear screen projection: The projector is set behind a special translucent screen. All projection equipment is hidden from the audience, causing a more dramatic presentation. The speaker is able to be near the screen and cords are hidden and taped. This has become the standard. A technician should be available in case of malfunctions. Projectors must be positioned correctly.

Standard projection: The use of any standard screen placed in front of the projector (including the following projectors).

Projectors

Overhead projector: This industry workhorse is still requested but is being rapidly replaced by the LCD (liquid crystal display; considered an overhead projector). It can be mounted on the ceiling or on a projection table and used with a laptop or PC, primarily to project Power Point slides and Web presentations.

Opaque Projector: This one reflects an image from paper material. It must be used from the rear of a dark room and must be cooled with a loud motor.

Slide Projector: 35mm carousel, mounted in standard frames that measure two inches square. The 35mm slide is the industry standard. Wireless remote control devices or laser pointers are now commonly used.

Note: Keep spare lamps for all projectors, fuses, and extension cords on hand. Wireless remote control devices or laser pointer are also now commonly used.

Videotape VCR Projectors: These projectors are used with a TV monitor to view VHS video. Most previous forms (Beta) are obsolete. DVD players: Available at most hotels with meeting facilities. (VHS tapes are no longer being made.) Players will become standard when film production facilities convert all former VHS tapes to this medium. Recordable DVDs have a much sharper picture than a videotape, which also wears out as it passes over the metal play heads. DVDs are touched only by a beam of light and should remain in good condition even after you play them thousands of times.

Strategies

Convention sales strategies focus on short and long term goals. In the short term, the next three years, our efforts will focus on close-in bookings to include regional and small corporate, association and tradeshow business that can be accommodated by our hotel community and limited use of the Convention Center. We aggressively pursue the large-scale shows understanding that booking patterns are typically a minimum of 3-5 years in the future.

To accomplish the above, the department will actively participate in RSCVA's numerous marketing & advertising campaigns/promotions.

In addition the sales staff's tasks consist of, but are not limited to the following:

1. Client appreciation events.
2. Client educational events.
3. Contacting prospective customers.
4. Courtesy and follow-up calls to existing customers, to ensure customer retention.
5. Development of community/hotel relationships.
6. Direct mail/data base management.
7. Familiarization Trip management.
8. Lead generation.
9. Membership in professional organizations.

10. Sales presentations.
11. Site inspections.
12. Trade show attendance.

Once the program has selected our area, the servicing department's tasks consist of, but are not limited to the following:

1. Assist in event marketing to build attendance.
2. Client solicitation to utilize our services.
3. Collateral management.
4. Daily management of an MINT, an industry software system that tracks group history and verifies organizational information for sales efforts.
5. Develop relationships with local businesses to promote their services to our clients.
6. Group coordination.
7. Preconvention meetings.
8. Postconvention meetings.
9. Registration personnel scheduling.
10. Tradeshow attendance to promote services.

Role of The Meeting Planner

Not long ago, just the ability to envision and somewhat successfully meander through logistics of a company meeting or event was acceptable. Not anymore. The meeting industry has become a $41.8 billion dollar affair and there are more than one million meetings held annually. And, the significance and value of a successful meeting planner has risen dramatically within the organizational structure. Today's planner possesses exceptional visionary and procedural skills, patience, and the drive and fortitude to execute strategic, effective meetings. Many of today's top executives are teaming that a meeting planner's contribution to a company's measured success is valid, valued and essential.

Meetings have a significant return on investment (ROI) for an organization's corporate mission, financial goals and a positive economic impact on host cities. The trend today (and for tomorrow) is to utilize corporate meetings as a prime revenue generator, strategic communications tool and a significant part of a company's marketing effort. For the meeting planner, proving a substantial, worthwhile return on investment provides job security and can enhance their status in the corporate hierarchy. Much like sales executives or business development personnel, a successful meeting planner is a business multiplier whose skills and importance can be neglected no longer.

For some businesses, this information and the value of it is not new. Successful execution of meetings and events already have had a significant, measurable impact on a multitude of different companies' bottom lines. Effective, positive, measurable and morale-enhancing meetings now are routinely part of a successful organization's annual strategic plan. The importance of a well-thought-out, finely tuned organizational meeting cannot be overstated and that all starts with a professional meeting planner.

Gone are the days when management deduced that meetings and conferences were something that "just happened every year or so." They are now viewed as quality forums where measurable ROI is tangible and real. Highly successful meetings finish at or under budget, achieve senior management's expectations, meet revenue projections to cover direct expenses and overhead costs, have a positive impact on the company's bottom line and enhance the branding perspective and overall mission.

Another example of the elevated role of the meeting planner is the opportunity for certification. Certified Meeting Professional (CMP) certification offers tactical instruction and certifies that the holder is knowledgeable of meeting and convention standards and has been responsible and accountable for successful meeting management. Acquiring this certification often yields industry and peer recognition and increased earning potential. Another program is Certification in Meeting Management (CMM). This certification is a university-endorsed professional designation for senior-level meeting professionals. Both certifications can differentiate the level of skill and knowledge between meeting planners and demonstrate the rising significance of the profession.

The rise and scope of meetings being held annually also is evidence of the importance of the meeting planner. According to recent research by Meeting Professionals International (MPI), overall there will be a nine percent increase in the number of meetings for 2001. Corporations will increase the number of meetings they hold annually by almost 15 percent. And, with the number of larger meetings increasing, the average lead-time for planners now is about two years. Smaller meetings usually require at least a six-month lead-time. With that, it's easy to see how this critical position has developed into a full-time responsibility and invaluable position within an organization.

Today's meeting planners do much more than manage events — they have a pivotal role in delivering marketing messages that impact a company's bottom-line. Meeting professionals are quickly becoming that cogent specialization (much like the information management officer of a few years ago) that an organization simply cannot do without. The advantages that a successful meeting can impart on a business often are measured and enjoyed for a long time. Evelyn Laxgang, CMP, is director of strategic programs and events for Motorola and the International Chairwoman of the Board of Meeting Professionals International.

9

Food and Beverage Service for Meetings

A number of on-site restaurants provide a variety of dining experiences, from casual poolside dining to the most elegant dinner accompanied by fine wines. Or dine in your room; it's all included in the package. Intimate dinner meetings or private parties can be arranged in any of the smaller rooms as well as banquets for the entire group.

Food and Beverage Serving and Related Workers

Food and beverage serving and related workers are the front line of customer service in full-service restaurants, casual dining eateries, and other food service establishments. These workers greet customers, escort them to seats and hand them menus, take food and drink orders, and serve food and beverages. They also answer questions, explain menu items and specials, and keep tables and dining areas clean and set for new diners. Most work as part of a team, helping coworkers to improve workflow and customer service.

Waiters and waitresses, also called *servers*, are the largest group of these workers. They take customers' orders, serve food and beverages, prepare itemized checks, and sometimes accept payment. Their specific duties vary considerably, depending on the establishment. In casual-dining restaurants serving routine, straightforward fare, such as salads, soups, and sandwiches, servers are expected to provide fast, efficient, and courteous service. In fine dining restaurants, where more complicated meals are prepared and often served over several courses, waiters and waitresses provide more formal service emphasizing personal, attentive treatment at a more leisurely pace. Waiters and waitresses may meet with managers and chefs before each shift to discuss the menu and any new items or specials, review ingredients for potential food allergies, or talk about any food safety concerns. They also discuss coordination between the kitchen and the dining room and any customer service issues from the previous day or shift. In addition, waiters and waitresses usually check the identification of patrons to ensure they meet the minimum age requirement for the purchase of alcohol and tobacco products wherever those items are sold.

Waiters and waitresses sometimes perform the duties of other food and beverage service workers, including escorting guests to tables, serving customers seated at counters, clearing and setting up tables, or operating a cash register. However, full-service restaurants frequently hire other staff, such as hosts and hostesses, cashiers, or dining room attendants, to perform these duties.

Bartenders fill drink orders either taken directly from patrons at the bar or through waiters and waitresses who place drink orders for dining room customers. Bartenders check the identification of customers seated at the bar to ensure they meet the minimum age requirement for the purchase of alcohol and tobacco products. They prepare mixed drinks, serve bottled or draught beer, and pour wine or other beverages. Bartenders must know a wide range of drink recipes and be able to mix drinks accurately, quickly, and without waste. Some establishments, especially those with higher volume, use equipment that automatically measures, pours, and mixes drinks at the push of a button. Bartenders who use this equipment, however, still must work quickly to handle a large volume of drink orders and be familiar with the ingredients for special drink requests. Much of a bartender's work still must be done by hand.

Besides mixing and serving drinks, bartenders stock and prepare garnishes for drinks; maintain an adequate supply of ice, glasses, and other bar supplies; and keep the bar area clean for customers. They also may collect payment, operate the cash register, wash glassware and utensils, and serve food to customers who dine at the bar. Bartenders usually are responsible for ordering and maintaining an inventory of liquor, mixers, and other bar supplies.

Hosts and hostesses welcome guests and maintain reservation and waiting lists. They may direct patrons to coatrooms, restrooms, or to a place to wait until their table is ready. Hosts and hostesses assign guests to tables suitable for the size of their group, escort patrons to their seats, and provide menus. They also enter reservations, arrange parties, and assist with other special requests. In some restaurants, they act as cashiers.

Dining room and cafeteria attendants and bartender helpers—sometimes referred to collectively as the bus staff—assist waiters, waitresses, and bartenders by cleaning and setting tables, removing dirty dishes, and keeping serving areas stocked with supplies. They may also assist waiters and waitresses by bringing meals out of the kitchen, distributing dishes to individual diners, filling water glasses, and delivering condiments. *Cafeteria attendants* stock serving tables with food, trays, dishes, and silverware. They may carry trays to dining tables for patrons. *Bartender helpers* keep bar equipment clean and glasses washed. *Dishwashers* clean dishes, cutlery, and kitchen utensils and equipment.

Food also is prepared and served in limited-service eateries, which don't employ servers and specialize in simpler preparations that often are made in advance. Two occupations with large numbers of workers are common in these types of establishments: *combined food preparation and serving workers, including fast food;* and *counter attendants, cafeteria, food concession, and coffee shop.* Combined food preparation and serving workers are employed primarily by fast food restaurants. They take food and beverage orders, retrieve items when ready, fill drink cups, and accept payment. They also may heat food items and assemble salads and sandwiches, which constitutes food preparation. Counter attendants take orders and serve food in snack bars, cafeterias, movie theatres, and coffee shops over a counter or steam table. They may fill cups with coffee, soda, and other beverages and may prepare fountain specialties, such as milkshakes and ice cream sundaes. Counter attendants take carryout orders from diners and wrap or place items in containers. They clean counters, write itemized bills, and sometimes accept payment. Other workers, referred to as *foodservers, nonrestaurant,* serve food to patrons outside of a restaurant environment. They might deliver room service meals in hotels or meals to hospital rooms or act as carhops, bringing orders to parked cars.

Work environment. Food and beverage service workers are on their feet most of the time and often carry heavy trays of food, dishes, and glassware. During busy dining periods, they are under pressure to serve customers quickly and efficiently. The work is relatively safe, but injuries from slips, cuts, and burns often result from hurrying or mishandling sharp tools. Three occupations—food servers, nonrestaurant; dining room and cafeteria attendants and bartender helpers; and dishwashers—reported higher incident rates than many occupations throughout the economy.

Part-time work is more common among food and beverage serving and related workers than among workers in almost any other occupation. In 2008, those on part-time schedules included half of all waiters and waitresses and almost three-fourths of all hosts and hostesses.

Food service and drinking establishments typically maintain long dining hours and offer flexible and varied work opportunities. Many food and beverage serving and related workers work evenings, weekends, and holidays. The long business hours allow for more flexible schedules that appeal to many teenagers who can gain valuable work experience. More than one-fifth of all food and beverage serving and related workers were 16 to 19 years old in 2008—about six times the proportion for all workers.

Training, Other Qualifications and Advancement

Most food and beverage service jobs are entry level and require a high school diploma or less. Generally, training is received on the job; however, those who wish to work at more upscale restaurants, where income from tips is greater and service standards are higher, may need previous experience or vocational training.

There are no specific educational requirements for most food and beverage service jobs. Many employers prefer to hire high school graduates for waiter and waitress, bartender, and host and hostess positions, but completion of high school usually is not required for fast-food workers, counter attendants, dishwashers, and dining room attendants and bartender helpers. Many entrants to these jobs are in their late teens or early twenties and have a high school education or less. Usually, they have little or no work experience. Food and beverage service jobs are a major source of part-time employment for high school and college students, multiple job holders, and those seeking supplemental incomes.

All new employees receive some training from their employer. They learn safe food handling procedures and sanitation practices, for example. Some employers, particularly those in fast-food restaurants, teach new workers using self-study programs, on-line programs, audiovisual presentations, and instructional booklets that explain food preparation and service skills. But most food and beverage serving and related workers pick up their skills by observing and working with more experienced workers. Some full-service restaurants also provide new dining room employees with some form of classroom training that alternates with periods of on-the-job work experience. These training programs communicate the operating philosophy of the restaurant, help establish a personal rapport with other staff, teach formal serving techniques, and instill a desire to work as a team. They also provide an opportunity to discuss customer service situations and the proper ways to handle unpleasant circumstances or unruly patrons.

Some food serving workers can acquire more skills by attending relevant classes offered by public or private vocational schools, restaurant associations, or large restaurant chains. Some bartenders acquire their skills through formal vocational training either by attending a school for bartending or a vocational and technical school where bartending classes are taught. These programs often include instruction on State and local laws and regulations, cocktail recipes, proper attire and conduct, and stocking a bar. Some of these schools help their graduates find jobs. Although few employers require any minimum level of educational attainment, some specialized training is usually needed in food handling and legal issues surrounding serving alcoholic beverages. Employers are more likely to hire and promote employees based on people skills and personal qualities than education.

Other qualifications. Restaurants rely on good food and customer service to retain loyal customers and succeed in a competitive industry. Food and beverage serving and related workers who exhibit excellent personal qualities—such as a neat appearance, an ability to work as part of a team, and a natural rapport with customers—will be highly sought after. Most States require workers who serve alcoholic beverages to be at least 18 years of age, but some States require servers to be older. For bartender jobs, many employers prefer to hire people who are 25 or older. All servers that serve alcohol need to be familiar with State and local laws concerning the sale of alcoholic beverages.

Waiters and waitresses need a good memory to avoid confusing customers' orders and to recall faces, names, and preferences of frequent patrons. Knowledge of a foreign language can be helpful to communicate with a diverse clientele and staff. Restaurants and hotels that have rigid table service standards often offer higher wages and have greater income potential from tips, but they may also have stiffer employment requirements, such as prior table service experience or higher education attainment than other establishments.

Due to the relatively small size of most food-serving establishments, opportunities for promotion are limited. After gaining experience, some dining room and cafeteria attendants and bartender helpers advance to waiter, waitress, or bartender jobs. For waiters, waitresses, and bartenders, advancement usually is limited to finding a job in a busier or more expensive restaurant or bar where prospects for tip earnings are better. Some bartenders, hosts and hostesses, and waiters and waitresses advance to supervisory jobs, such as dining room supervisor, maitre d', assistant manager, or restaurant general manager. A few bartenders open their own businesses. In larger restaurant chains, food and beverage service workers who excel often are invited to enter the company's formal management training program. (For more information, see food service managers elsewhere in the *Handbook*.)

EMPLOYMENT

Food and beverage serving and related workers held 7.7 million jobs in 2008. The distribution of jobs among the various food and beverage serving occupations was as follows:

Occupation	Jobs
Combined food preparation and serving workers, including fast food	2,701,700
Waiters and waitresses	2,381,600
Counter attendants, cafeteria, food concession, and coffee shop	525,400
Dishwashers	522,900
Bartenders	508,700
Dining room and cafeteria attendants and bartender helpers	420,700
Hosts and hostesses, restaurant, lounge, and coffee shop	350,700
Food servers, nonrestaurant	189,800
All other food preparation and serving related workers	50,900

The overwhelming majority of jobs for food and beverage serving and related workers were found in food services and drinking places, such as restaurants, fast food outlets, bars, and catering or contract food service operations. Other jobs were in hotels, motels, and other traveler accommodation establishments; amusement, gambling, and recreation establishments; educational services; nursing care facilities; and civic and social organizations.

Jobs are located throughout the country but are more plentiful in larger cities and tourist areas. Vacation resorts offer seasonal employment.

Earnings

Food and beverage serving and related workers derive their earnings from a combination of hourly wages and customer tips. Earnings vary greatly, depending on the type of job and establishment. For example, fast-food workers and hosts and hostesses usually do not receive tips, so their wage rates may be higher than those of waiters and waitresses and bartenders in full-service restaurants, but their overall earnings might be lower. In many full-service restaurants, tips are higher than wages. In some restaurants, workers contribute all or a portion of their tips to a tip pool, which is distributed among qualifying workers. Tip pools allow workers who don't usually receive tips directly from customers, such as dining room attendants, to feel a part of a team and to share in the rewards of good service.

In May 2008, median hourly wages (including tips) of waiters and waitresses were $8.01. The middle 50 percent earned between $7.32 and $10.35. The lowest 10 percent earned less than $6.73, and the highest 10 percent earned more than $14.26 an hour. For most waiters and waitresses, higher earnings are primarily the result of receiving more in tips rather than higher hourly wages. Tips usually average between 10 percent and 20 percent of guests' checks; waiters and waitresses working in busy or expensive restaurants earn the most.

Bartenders had median hourly wages (including tips) of $8.54. The middle 50 percent earned between $7.53 and $10.98. The lowest 10 percent earned less than $7.00, and the highest 10 percent earned more than $14.93 an hour. Like waiters and waitresses, bartenders employed in public bars may receive more than half of their earnings as tips. Service bartenders often are paid higher hourly wages to offset their lower tip earnings.

Median hourly wages (including tips) of dining room and cafeteria attendants and bartender helpers were $8.05. The middle 50 percent earned between $7.39 and $9.44. The lowest 10 percent earned less than $6.82, and the highest 10 percent earned more than $11.67 an hour. Most received over half of their earnings as wages; the rest of their income was a share of the proceeds from tip pools.

Median hourly wages of hosts and hostesses were $8.42. The middle 50 percent earned between $7.50 and $9.70. The lowest 10 percent earned less than $6.88, and the highest 10 percent earned more than $11.89 an hour. Wages comprised the majority of their earnings. In some cases, wages were supplemented by proceeds from tip pools.

Median hourly wages of combined food preparation and serving workers, including fast food, were $7.90. The middle 50 percent earned between $7.26 and $9.12. The lowest 10 percent earned less than $6.67, and the highest 10 percent earned more than $10.67 an hour. Although some combined food preparation and serving workers receive a part of their earnings as tips, fast-food workers usually do not.

Median hourly wages of counter attendants in cafeterias, food concessions, and coffee shops (including tips) were $8.42. The middle 50 percent earned between $7.57 and $9.64 an hour. The lowest 10 percent earned less than $6.97, and the highest 10 percent earned more than $11.73 an hour.

Median hourly wages of dishwashers were $8.19. The middle 50 percent earned between $7.47 and $9.35. The lowest 10 percent earned less than $6.90, and the highest 10 percent earned more than $10.74 an hour.

Median hourly wages of food servers outside of restaurants were $9.32. The middle 50 percent earned between $7.93 and $11.64. The lowest 10 percent earned less than $7.20, and the highest 10 percent earned more than $14.69 an hour.

Many beginning or inexperienced workers earn the Federal minimum wage ($7.25 per hour as of July 24, 2009), but many States set minimum wages higher than the Federal minimum. Also, various minimum wage exceptions apply under specific circumstances to disabled workers, full-time students, youth under age 20 in their first 90 days of employment, tipped employees, and student-learners. Tipped employees are those who customarily and regularly receive more than $30 a month in tips. The employer may consider tips as part of wages, but the employer must pay at least $2.13 an hour in direct wages.

Many employers provide free meals and furnish uniforms, but some may deduct from wages the cost, or fair value, of any meals or lodging provided. Food and beverage service workers who work full time often receive typical benefits, but part-time workers usually do not. In some large restaurants and hotels, food and beverage serving and related workers belong to unions—principally the Unite HERE and the Service Employees International Union.

Clubs

Clubs, as a sector of the hotel and catering industry, are establishments offering food and drink, with at times accommodation, to members and bonafide guests. The types of clubs varying from working men's clubs, to political party clubs, social clubs, sporting clubs, restaurant clubs, to the private exclusive clubs.

Basically, in England and Wales, clubs are of two main types :

(a) Proprietary clubs : These are licensed clubs, owned by individuals or company and operated by themselves for self-profit, and as such require a Justice's Licence to operate. It is usual for a high proportion of proprietary clubs to resemble licensed restaurants with a substantial part of their turnover obtained from the sales of food.

(b) Registered clubs : These are registered clubs in which the management is responsible to an elected committee; the members own all the property including the food and drink, and pay their subscriptions to a common fund. As a non-profit making club which belongs to all the members and provides a service to the members, it is a genuine members' club and does not require a Justice's Licence to operate. It requires to be registered. The turnover of the members' clubs is mainly obtained from the sale of drinks which are normally sold at a competitive price as the profit element in clubs is lower than say in public houses.

Restaurants And Snack Bars

Unlike the hotel facilities already described, commercial restaurants do not offer accommodation and therefore their primary function is the provision of food and beverage. Because these restaurants do not have any in-house trade they are very reliant on passing trade and the reputation they develop from word-of-mouth advertising.

The various types of restaurants include snack bars, cafes, coffee shops, take-aways, steak bars, speciality restaurants, haute cuisine restaurants, etc. These diverse types of restaurants have service-styles, ranging from the self-service catering to the more elaborate methods of table service (e.g. French, Russian, English) found in luxury restaurants, and those particular service techniques specific to speciality restaurants such as Chinese, Polynesian and Indian.

In many restaurants today separate bar areas are provided for pre and after-meal drinks. These have the double advantage of offering the customer a place to sit and relax away from the dining area and they allow a faster seat turn-over in the restaurant.

Public Houses

Public Houses consist of a varied group of establishments, which mainly offer the general public alcohlic liquor for sale for consumption on and off the premises. The supply of food, at one time ancillary to liquor, is been seen more in recent years as a very important element in the 'product' for the consumer. The characteristics of public houses are, firstly, that they all require a licence to operate and that the licence is only granted to suitable persons, and secondly, that most public houses are owned by a brewery company, providing an integration of their production with the retail distribution of alcoholic beverages.

In order to become more competitive, to meet customers demands, the catering premises in most pubs have improved considerably in recent years. Some brewer companies have classified their public houses by the level of catering offered. This ranges from those offering just sandwiches to hot and cold snacks, to a cold buffet counter, to a bistro-type operation, to a griddle or steak bar to a full a la carte menu. The range of food items offered mainly being of the convenience food type but at times extending to fresh food items. Several brewery companies market specific pubs, by the type of catering offered, with a brand image, *e.g.* Beefeater Steak houses.

Subsidized Or Welfare Sector

Subsidized or welfare food and beverage establishments may be defined as those operations in which the profitability of the catering facility is the outlet's primary concern. Since the operations are either completely or partially subsidized by a parent body, such establishment's primary obligation is the well-being and care or their customers or patients. Unlike customers frequenting commercial sector operations, these customers often do not have a choice of catering facilities, for *e.g.* in hospitals and schools. Non-commercial operations are usually subsidized by government bodies which dictate an allowance per head, or by parent companies who may have a similar arrangement.

A distinction can be made between institutional catering and employee catering facilities, *e.g.* in hospitals and schools. Non-commercial operations embraces catering in institutions such as prisons, schools, hospitals. An important characteristic of this type of catering is that the market is not only restricted to the inmates of the institutions but in most cases it is also captive. In addition, in most cases, institutional catering is completely subsidized. Employee catering may be in the public or private ownership and covers the provision of food and beverage services to employees. The degree of subsidy in this type of operation varies considerably and also in many cases the market is not entirely captive. In other words, the catering outlet may be competing with the catering facilities provided at nearby restaurants, pubs and take-aways or with food brought in by the workers from their homes.

Institutional Catering

Institutional catering establishments include schools, universities, colleges hospitals, the Services, and prisons. In some of these establishments certain groups of customers do not have to pay for the provision of the food and beverage services as they are completely or partially subsidized by various government funds. This part of the catering industry is commonly referred to as the welfare sector. Very few catering contractors are found in this sector so the majority are self-operated.

Schools

The school meals catering service was until recently structured on a dietary basis with a daily or weekly per capital allowance to ensure that the children obtained adequate nutritional levels from their meals. Most of the schools used to operate their dining rooms on a family-type-serve or a self-service basis with the traditional 'Meat and two veg' lunch being very much the norm. There is today, however, a trend of provision of a snack-type lunch as an alternative to a main meal. Some schools now provide sandwiches, rolls, pies, soups, yoghurts, etc., and the children may choose from this selection. This trend has gone one step further in some areas which have drastically cut their school meal service and are providing more of the dining room space for the children to bring in their own lunches from home. Whether this trend will continue and spread in the future, or whether it is merely a current 'fad' is a debatable issue. It does seem likely, however, that now introduced, the snack-type meal will at least remain as an alternative to the traditional school meal.

A further trend since 1983 has been for some local education authorities hire specialist contract caterers.

Universities And Colleges

The public sector universities and local education authority institutions such as polytechnics, colleges of education and colleges of further education provide catering facilities for the academic, administrative, technical and secretarial staff as well as for full-and part-time students and visitors. The catering service in this sector of the industry suffers from an under-utilization of it's facilities during the three vacation periods and also in many instances at the weekends.

Universities are autonomous bodies and are responsible for their own catering services. They are, however, publicly accountable for the expenditure to the University Grants Committee (UGC) which allocates the funds on behalf of the Exchequer. The UGC's policy on catering allows for a subsidy on capital costs, *i.e.* "Buildings and equipment, Landlord expenses and rent and rates where applicable". Apart from a few special exemptions to certain universities, they are expected to break even. University catering units have traditionally been of two basic kinds :

1. Residential facilities attached to halls which serve breakfast and evening meals.
2. The central facilities which are open to all students and staff and usually serve lunches and snacks throughout the day with beverage. These catering facilities have to openly compete with the students's union services and independently-staffed senior common rooms.

The residential students pay in advance for part or in total for their board and lodgings. This method has been abandoned by many universities in recent years who have provided limited kitchen facilities in the residences to enable students to prepare and cook their own meals if they wished to and also introduced a pay-as you-eat system for residential students. Unfortunately, this introduction has reduced the catering revenue from students who prepare and cook their own meals.

To offset the losses incurred and to achieve a position of breakeven in catering, universities often utilize their residential and catering facilities by making them available at commercial rates to outside bodies for meetings, conferences and for holidays during the vacation periods.

Polytechnics, colleges of education and colleges of further education are financed by the local education authorities. There is no overall objective catering policy and the practices vary from one institution to another depending very much on the local authority and the local political party in power. In general most polytechnics and colleges catering is subsidized with policies usually requiring that food and labour costs be covered for the year from the catering revenue, by accepting losses in the summer term because of circumstances requiring lower student attendance and by making a gross profit during the rest of the year.

Hospitals

Hospital catering facilities have improved considerably over the past twenty years with the result that new hospitals in particular are benefiting from the well-planned and managed catering services. Hospitals require a specialized form of catering as the customer is normally unable to move elsewhere and choose alternative facilities and therefore special attention must be given to the food and beverage. As with the school meals service, the hospital catering service is structured on a per capital allowance for patients but with staff paying for all of their meals.

Traditionally, a decentralized approach was used in the hospital in which the patient's food and beverage were portioned away from the main production area, at the hospital's kitchens and wards. This, of course resulted however, in the patients receiving cold, unappetizing meals because of the length of time between the food being prepared and the patients actually receiving it. Today this method of food service is being replaced by the centralized approach which involves the preparation of the patients' trays in or close to the main production area. From here they are transported by trucks or mechanical conveyors to various floors, and from there directly to the patients so that there is very little delay between the food being plated and served to the patient.

A recent trend, though, has been for hospital catering to be open for tender by contract caterers where in many instances a general production system for several nearby hospitals would have to be operated to be viable.

The Services

The Services include the Armed Forces—the Navy, Army and Air Force; the Police and Fire service; and some government departments. In the Armed Forces they often have their own specialist catering brand for example the Army has the Army Catering Corps, and civil organisation such as the Metropolitan Police force and the Post Office service also their own catering departments. The levels of food and beverage facilities for the Services vary from the large self-service cafeterias for the majority of personnel, to the high-class traditional restaurants for the more senior members of staff. A considerable number of functions are also held by the Services giving rise to both small and large scale banquet arrangements.

Bibliography

- Aguilera, Jose Miguel and David W. Stanley. Microstructural Principles of Food Processing and Engineering. Springer, 1999. ISBN 0-8342-1256-0.
- Campbell, Bernard Grant. Human Evolution: An Introduction to Man's Adaptations. Aldine Transaction: 1998. ISBN 0-202-02042-8.
- Carpenter, Ruth Ann; Finley, Carrie E. Healthy Eating Every Day. Human Kinetics, 2005. ISBN 0-7360-5186-4.
- Clifford J. Routes (1999). Travel and Translation in the Late Twentieth Century. Cambridge, MA: Harvard University Press.
- Digital Equipment Corporation (1972) (PDF). PDP-11/40 Processor Handbook. Maynard, MA: Digital Equipment Corporation.
- Howe, P. and S. Devereux. Famine Intensity and Magnitude Scales: A Proposal for an Instrumental Definition of Famine. 2004.
- Humphery, Kim. Shelf Life: Supermarkets and the Changing Cultures of Consumption. Cambridge University Press, 1998. ISBN 0-521-62630-7.
- Immanuel Velikovsky (1982). Mankind in Amnesia. Garden City, New York: Doubleday.
- John B. Switzer (2007). "Hospitality" in Encyclopedia of Love in World Religions. Santa Barbara, CA: ABC-CLIO.
- Kempf, Karl (1961). Historical Monograph: Electronic Computers Within the Ordnance Corps. Aberdeen Proving Ground (United States Army).

- Lavington, Simon (1998). A History of Manchester Computers (2 ed.). Swindon: The British Computer Society. ISBN 0902505018
- Lawrie, Stephen; R A Lawrie. Lawrie's Meat Science. Woodhead Publishing: 1998. ISBN 1-85573-395-1.
- Magdoff, Fred; Foster, John Bellamy; and Buttel, Frederick H. Hungry for Profit: The Agribusiness Threat to Farmers, Food, and the Environment. September 2000. ISBN 1-58367-016-5.
- McGee, Harold. On Food and Cooking: The Science and Lore of the Kitchen. New York: Simon and Schuster, 2004. ISBN 0-684-80001-2.
- Mead, Margaret. The Changing Significance of Food. In Carole Counihan and Penny Van Esterik (Ed.), Food and Culture: A Reader. UK: Routledge, 1997. ISBN 0-415-91710-7.
- Merson, Michael H.; Black, Robert E.; Mills, Anne J. International Public Health: Disease, Programs, Systems, and Policies. Jones and Bartlett Publishers, 2005.
- Meuer, Hans; Strohmaier, Erich; Simon, Horst; Dongarra, Jack (2006-11-13). "Architectures Share Over Time". TOP500.
- Mireille Rosello (2001). Postcolonial Hospitality. The Immigrant as Guest. Standford, CA: Stanford University Press.
- Nicklas, Barbara J. Endurance Exercise and Adipose Tissue. CRC Press, 2002. ISBN 0-8493-0460-1.
- Parekh, Sarad R. The Gmo Handbook: Genetically Modified Animals, Microbes, and Plants in Biotechnology. Humana Press,2004. ISBN 1-58829-307-6.
- Petersen, Glen S. (2008). The Profit Maximization Paradox: Cracking the Marketing/Sales Alignment Code. Booksurge Llc. pp. 176. ISBN 9781419691799.
- Phillips, Tony (2000). "The Antikythera Mechanism I". American Mathematical Society.
- Verma, G.; Mielke, N. (1988). Reliability performance of ETOX based flash memories. IEEE International Reliability Physics Symposium.
- Wood Thorogood, Pelin and Gschwandtner, Gerhard. InsideCRM, Nov 25, 2008 "Sales 2.0: How Will It Improve Your Business?"

Index

N

O

P

R

S

T

U

V

W